CW00456696

CONGREGATION FOR DIVINE WORSHIP AND
THE DISCIPLINE OF THE SACRAMENTS

HOMILETIC DIRECTORY

VATICAN CITY 2014

*All documents are published thanks to the generous support
of the members of the Catholic Truth Society*

CATHOLIC TRUTH SOCIETY
PUBLISHERS TO THE HOLY SEE

First published 2015 by The Incorporated Catholic Truth Society 40-46 Harleyford Road London SE11 5AY Tel: 020 7640 0042   Fax: 020 7640 0046. Copyright © 2014 Libreria Editrice Vaticana, Citta del Vaticano. This edition © 2015 The Incorporated Catholic Truth Society.

ISBN 978 1 78469 052 6

ABBREVIATIONS

CCC   *Catechism of the Catholic Church*

DV   Second Vatican Council, Dogmatic Constitution on Divine Revelation *Dei Verbum*

EG   Apostolic Exhortation of Pope Francis *Evangelii Gaudium*

OLM   *Ordo Lectionum Missae, Praenotanda (Introduction of the Lectionary)*

SC   Second Vatican Council, Constitution on the Sacred Liturgy *Sacrosanctum Concilium*

VD   Apostolic Exhortation of Benedict XVI *Verbum Domini*

Prot. N. 531/14

DECREE

It is very poignant that Pope Francis wished to devote considerable attention to the theme of the *homily* in his Apostolic Exhortation *Evangelii Gaudium*. Both positive and negative aspects of the state of preaching had already been expressed by Bishops gathered in Synod, and guidance for homilists was offered in the Post-Synodal Apostolic Exhortations *Verbum Domini* and *Sacramentum Caritatis* of Pope Benedict XVI.

From this perspective, and bearing in mind the provisions of the Constitution on the Sacred Liturgy *Sacrosanctum Concilium*, as well as subsequent Magisterial teaching, and in light of the *Introduction of the Lectionary for Mass* and the *General Instruction of the Roman Missal*, this two-part *Homiletic Directory* has been prepared.

In the first part, entitled *The homily and its liturgical setting*, the nature, function, and specific context of the homily are described. Other aspects that define it are also addressed, namely, the appropriate ordained minister who delivers it, its reference to the Word of God, the proximate and remote preparation for its composition, and its recipients.

In the second part, the *Ars praedicandi*, essential questions of method and content that the homilist must know and take into account in the preparation and delivery of the homily are illustrated. In a way that is meant to be indicative and not exhaustive, interpretive keys are proposed for the cycle of Sundays and Feasts, beginning at the heart of the liturgical year (the Sacred Triduum and Easter Time, Lent, Advent, Christmas Time, and Ordinary Time), and also for the Masses of weekdays, weddings, and funerals. In these examples, the criteria outlined in the first part of the Directory are put into practice: typology between the Old and New Testaments, the importance of the Gospel reading, the ordering of the readings, and the nexus between the Liturgy of the Word and the Liturgy of the Eucharist, between the Biblical message and the liturgical texts, between celebration and life, and between listening to God and the particular assembly.

Two appendices follow the main text. In the first, with the intention of showing the link between the homily and the doctrine of the Catholic Church, references are given to the Catechism according to various doctrinal themes in the readings for each of the Sundays and Feasts of the three year cycle. In the second appendix, references to various Magisterial teachings on the homily are provided.

This text was presented to each of the Fathers of the Congregation for Divine Worship and the Discipline of the Sacraments, and was reviewed and approved at the Ordinary Sessions of 7th February and 20th May 2014. It was then presented to Pope Francis, who approved the publication of the *Homiletic Directory*. This Congregation is pleased, therefore, to make it available, desiring that "the homily can actually be an intense and happy experience of the Spirit, a consoling encounter with God's word, a constant source of renewal and growth" (*Evangelii Gaudium*, 135). Each homilist, making his own the sentiments of the Apostle Paul, is to renew the understanding that "as we have been approved by God to be entrusted with the gospel, so we speak, not to please men, but to please God who tests our hearts" (*1 Thess* 2:4).

Translations into the principal languages have been undertaken by this Dicastery, while translations into other languages remain the responsibility of the concerned Conferences of Bishops.

All things to the contrary notwithstanding.

From the offices of the Congregation for Divine Worship and the Discipline of the Sacraments, 29th June 2014, the Solemnity of Saints Peter and Paul, Apostles.

(Antonio Card. Cañizares Llovera)
Prefect

(✠ Arthur Roche)
Archbishop Secretary

TABLE OF CONTENTS

INTRODUCTION

1. This *Homiletic Directory* has been produced as the result of the request made by participants in the Synod of Bishops held in 2008 on the Word of God. In response to this request, Pope Benedict XVI directed the competent authorities to prepare a Directory on the homily (cf. VD 60). He had already made his own the concern of the Fathers of an earlier Synod that greater attention be given to the preparation of homilies (cf. *Sacramentum Caritatis* 46). His successor, Pope Francis, also considers preaching to be one of the priorities in the life of the Church, as is evident in his first Apostolic Exhortation, *Evangelii Gaudium.*

In describing the homily, the Fathers of the Second Vatican Council emphasised the unique nature of preaching in the context of the sacred liturgy: "The sermon [...] should draw its content mainly from scriptural and liturgical sources, and its character should be that of a proclamation of God's wonderful works in the history of salvation, the mystery of Christ, ever made present and active within us, especially in the celebration of the liturgy" (SC 35, 2). For many centuries the sermon was often a moral or doctrinal instruction delivered at Mass on Sundays and holy days, but it was not necessarily integrated into the celebration itself. Just as the Catholic liturgical movement that began in the late nineteenth century sought to re-integrate personal piety and liturgical spirituality among the faithful, so there were efforts to deepen the integral bond between the Scriptures and worship. These efforts, encouraged by the Popes throughout the first half of the twentieth century, bore fruit in the vision of the Church's liturgy bequeathed to us by the Second Vatican Council. The nature and purpose of the homily is to be understood from this perspective.

2. For the past fifty years many facets of the homily as envisioned by the Council have been explored in both the magisterial teaching of the Church and in the daily experience of those who exercise the preaching office. The aim of this Directory is to present the purpose of the homily as this has been described in the documents of the Church from the Second Vatican Council to the Apostolic Exhortation *Evangelii Gaudium*, and to offer guidance based on these resources to help preachers carry out

their mission properly and effectively. An Appendix at the end of the Directory brings together references to the relevant documents, and these demonstrate how the understanding of the Council has to some extent taken root and grown over the past half century. But they also indicate that further reflection is necessary to ensure the kind of preaching envisioned by the Council.

By way of introduction, we might note four important themes of perennial importance described briefly in the conciliar documents. First, of course, is the place of the Word of God in the liturgical celebration, and what this means regarding the purpose of the homily (cf. SC 24, 35, 52, 56). Second, there are the principles of Catholic biblical interpretation enunciated by the Council, which find a particular expression in the liturgical homily (cf. DV 9-13, 21). Third, there is the consequence of this understanding of the Bible and the liturgy for the preacher, which should shape not only his approach to preparing a homily, but his whole spiritual life (cf. DV 25; *Presbyterorum Ordinis* 4, 18). Fourth, there are the needs of those to whom the Church's preaching is directed, their culture and circumstances, which also determine the form of the homily, so that its hearers might be more deeply converted to the Gospel (cf. *Ad Gentes* 6). These brief but important directives have influenced Catholic preaching in the decades since the Council; their insights have found concrete expression in Church legislation and have been richly developed by papal teaching, as the citations in this *Directory* will clearly demonstrate, as well as the list of relevant documents included in Appendix II.

3. This *Homiletic Directory* seeks to assimilate the insights of the past fifty years, review them critically, help preachers appreciate the purpose of the homily, and offer them assistance in fulfilling a mission which is vital to the life of the Church. The focus is primarily the homily of the Sunday Eucharist, but what is said here applies, *mutatis mutandis,* to the preaching that ordinarily forms a part of every sacramental and liturgical celebration. Of necessity, the suggestions presented here must be general: the homily is a dimension of ministry that is especially variable, both because of the cultural differences from one congregation to another, and because of the gifts and limitations of the individual preacher. Every homilist wants to preach better, and at times the many demands of pastoral care and a sense of personal inadequacy can lead to discouragement. It is

true that some people are, by talent and training, more effective public speakers than others. But a feeling of personal limitation in this regard can be offset when we recall that Moses had a speech impediment (*Ex* 4:10), that Jeremiah thought himself too young to preach (*Jer* 1:6), and that Paul, by his own admission, experienced fear and trepidation (*1 Cor* 2:2-4). It is not necessary to be a great orator in order to be an effective homilist. Naturally, the art of oratory or public speaking, including the appropriate use of the voice and even of gesture, is an ingredient of a successful homily. While this matter is beyond the scope of this *Directory*, it is an important part of what a homilist needs to attend to. What is essential, however, is that the preacher makes the Word of God central to his own spiritual life, that he knows his people well, that he is reflective on the events of the times, that he continually seeks to develop the skills that help him preach effectively and above all, that in his spiritual poverty, he invites in faith the Holy Spirit as the principal agent that makes the hearts of the faithful amenable to the divine mysteries. Pope Francis exhorts preachers: "Let us renew our confidence in preaching, based on the conviction that it is God who seeks to reach out to others through the preacher, and that he displays his power through human words" (EG 136).

PART ONE:

THE HOMILY AND
ITS LITURGICAL SETTING

I. THE HOMILY

4. The unique nature of the homily is captured well in St Luke's account of Christ's preaching in the synagogue of Nazareth (cf. *Lk* 4:16-30). After reading a passage from the Prophet Isaiah he handed the scroll back to the attendant and began, "Today this scripture has been fulfilled in your hearing" (*Lk* 4:21). When we read this passage reflectively, we can sense the excitement that filled that small synagogue: to proclaim God's Word in the sacred assembly is an event. As we read in *Verbum Domini*: "... the liturgy is the privileged setting in which God speaks to us in the midst of our lives; he speaks today to his people, who hear and respond" (52). It is a privileged setting, although it is not the only setting. Certainly, God speaks to us in many ways: through the events in our lives, through our personal study of Scripture, in times of quiet prayer. But the liturgy is a privileged setting because it is there that we listen to God's Word as part of the celebration that culminates in the sacrificial offering of Christ to the eternal Father. The *Catechism* states that "the Eucharist makes the Church" (CCC 1396), but also that the Eucharist is inseparable from the Word of God (cf. CCC 1346).

Because the homily is an integral part of the liturgy, it is not only an instruction, it is also an act of worship. When we read the homilies of the Fathers, we find that many of them concluded their discourse with a doxology and the word "Amen": they understood that the purpose of the homily was not only to sanctify the people, but to glorify God. The homily is a hymn of gratitude for the *magnalia Dei*, which not only tells those assembled that God's Word is fulfilled in their hearing, but praises God for this fulfilment.

Given its liturgical nature, the homily also possesses a sacramental significance: Christ is present in the assembly gathered to listen to his word and in the preaching of his minister, through whom the same Lord who spoke long ago in the synagogue at Nazareth now instructs his people. In the words of *Verbum Domini*: "The sacramentality of the Word can thus be understood by analogy with the real presence of Christ under the appearances of the consecrated bread and wine. By approaching the altar and partaking in the Eucharistic banquet we truly share in the body and blood of Christ. The proclamation of God's word at the celebration entails an acknowledgement that Christ himself is present, that he speaks to us, and that he wishes to be heard" (VD 56).

5. It is because the homily is an integral part of the Church's worship that it is to be delivered only by bishops, priests, or deacons. So intimate is the bond between the table of the Word and the table of the altar that it is fitting that "The Homily should be given by the priest celebrant himself" (*General Instruction of the Roman Missal* 66), or, in any case, always by one ordained to preside or assist at the altar. Well-trained lay leaders can also give solid instruction and moving exhortation, and opportunities for such presentations should be provided in other contexts; but it is the intrinsically *liturgical* nature of the homily that demands that it be given only by those ordained to lead the Church's worship (cf. *Redemptionis Sacramentum* 161).

6. Pope Francis observes that the homily "is a distinctive genre, since it is preaching situated within the framework of the liturgical celebration; hence it should be brief and avoid taking on the semblance of a speech or lecture" (EG 138). The liturgical nature of the homily sheds light on its unique purpose. In considering this purpose, it might be helpful to say what the homily is not.

It is not a sermon on an abstract topic; in other words, the Mass is not an occasion for the preacher to address some issue completely unrelated to the liturgical celebration and its readings, or to do violence to the texts provided by the Church by twisting them to fit some preconceived idea. Nor is the homily simply an exercise in biblical exegesis. The people of God have a great hunger to explore the Scriptures, and pastors should provide them with opportunities and resources that enable them to deepen their knowledge of God's Word. However, the Sunday homily is not the occasion for in-depth biblical exegesis: there is not the time to do this well, and more importantly the homilist is called to proclaim how God's word is being fulfilled here and now. Next, the homily is not catechetical instruction, even if catechesis is an important dimension of the homily. As with biblical exegesis, there is not the time to do this properly; furthermore, this would represent a variation on the practice of presenting a discourse at Mass that is not really integral to the liturgical celebration itself. Finally, the time for the homily should not be taken up with the preacher's personal witness. There is no question that people can be deeply moved by personal stories, but the homily should express the faith of the Church, and not simply the preacher's own story. As Pope Francis warns, preaching that is purely moralistic, doctrinaire, or simply a lecture on biblical exegesis detracts from the heart-to-heart communication which should take place in the homily, and which possesses a quasi-sacramental character, because faith comes from what is heard (cf. EG 142).

7. In saying that the homily is none of these things, this does not mean that topical themes, biblical exegesis, doctrinal instruction, and personal witness have no place in preaching; indeed, they can be effective as *elements* in a good homily. It is very appropriate for a preacher to relate the texts of a particular celebration to the events and questions of the day, to share the fruits of scholarship in understanding a passage of Scripture and to demonstrate the connection between the Word of God and the doctrine of the Church. Like fire, all of these things make good servants but poor masters: if they serve the purpose of the homily, they are good; if they take the place of the homily, they are not. Furthermore, the preacher needs to speak in such a way that his hearers can sense his belief in the power of God. He must not lower the standards of his message to the level of his own personal witness, fearing that he will be accused of not practising what he preaches. Since he is preaching not himself, but Christ, he can, without hypocrisy, point out the heights of sanctity, to which, like every other individual, in his pilgrim faith he is aspiring.

8. It should also be emphasised that the homily should be tailored to the needs of the particular community, and indeed draw inspiration from it. Pope Francis speaks eloquently to this point in *Evangelii Gaudium*:

> The same Spirit who inspired the Gospels and who acts in the Church also inspires the preacher to hear the faith of God's people and to find the right way to preach at each Eucharist. Christian preaching thus

13

finds in the heart of people and their culture a source of living water, which helps the preacher to know what must be said and how to say it. Just as all of us like to be spoken to in our mother tongue, so too in the faith we like to be spoken to in our "mother culture," our native language (cf. *2 Macc* 7:21, 27), and our heart is better disposed to listen. This language is a kind of music which inspires encouragement, strength and enthusiasm (139).

9. What, then, is the homily? Two brief selections from the *Praenotanda* of the Church's liturgical books begin to answer this question. First, in the *General Instruction of the Roman Missal* we read:

> The homily is part of the Liturgy and is strongly recommended, for it is necessary for the nurturing of the Christian life. It should be an exposition of some aspect of the readings from Sacred Scripture or of another text from the Ordinary or from the Proper of the Mass of the day and should take into account both the mystery being celebrated and the particular needs of the listeners (65).

10. The *Introduction of the Lectionary* expands somewhat on this brief description:

> Through the course of the liturgical year the homily sets forth the mysteries of faith and the standards of the Christian life on the basis of the sacred text. [...] The purpose of the homily at Mass is that the spoken word of God and the liturgy of the Eucharist may together become "a proclamation of God's wonderful works in the history of salvation, the mystery of Christ" [SC 35, 2]. Through the readings and homily Christ's Paschal Mystery is proclaimed; through the sacrifice of the Mass it becomes present. Moreover Christ himself is always present and active in the preaching of his Church.

> Whether the homily explains the text of the Sacred Scriptures proclaimed in the readings or some other text of the Liturgy, it must always lead the community of the faithful to celebrate the Eucharist actively, "so that they may hold fast in their lives to what they have grasped by faith" [SC 10]. From this living explanation, the Word of God proclaimed in the readings and the Church's celebration of the

day's Liturgy will have greater impact. But this demands that the homily be truly the fruit of meditation, carefully prepared, neither too long nor too short, and suited to all those present, even children and the uneducated (OLM 24).

11. A few fundamental points should be underscored in these two descriptions. In the broadest sense, the homily is a discourse about the mysteries of faith and the standards of Christian life in a way suited to the particular needs of the listeners. This is a concise description of many kinds of preaching and exhortation. The specific form of the homily is suggested by the words "on the basis of the sacred text," which refers to the biblical passages *and* the prayers used in a liturgical celebration. This point should not be overlooked, because the prayers provide a useful hermeneutic for the preacher's interpretation of the biblical texts. What distinguishes a homily from other forms of instruction is its *liturgical context*. This understanding becomes crucial when the setting for the homily is the Eucharistic celebration: what the documents say here is essential to a proper understanding of the purpose of the homily. The Liturgy of the Word and the Liturgy of the Eucharist together proclaim God's wonderful work of our salvation in Christ: "… through the readings and homily Christ's Paschal Mystery is proclaimed; through the sacrifice of the Mass it becomes present." The homily at Mass "must always lead the community of the faithful to celebrate the Eucharist actively, 'so that they may hold fast in their lives to what they have grasped through faith' [SC 10]" (OLM 24).

12. This description of the homily at Mass suggests a simple yet challenging dynamic. The first movement is suggested by the words: "through the readings and homily Christ's Paschal Mystery is proclaimed." The preacher speaks about the readings and prayers of the celebration in such a way that their meaning is found in the death and Resurrection of the Lord. It is striking how closely "the readings and homily" are associated in this formulation, to the point that a poor proclamation of the biblical readings can adversely affect the understanding of the homily. *Both* are proclamation, and this underscores once again how the homily is a *liturgical* act; indeed, it is a sort of extension of the proclamation of the readings themselves. In connecting the readings with the Paschal Mystery, the reflection could well touch on doctrinal or moral teaching suggested by the texts.

13. The second movement is suggested by the words: "through the sacrifice of the Mass it [the Paschal Mystery] becomes present." The second part of the homily prepares the community to celebrate the Eucharist, and to recognise that in this celebration they truly share in the mystery of the Lord's death and Resurrection. Virtually every homily could be conceived as implicitly needing to say again the words of the Apostle Paul: "The cup of benediction that we bless, is it not a communion in the Blood of Christ? And the bread that we break, is it not a participation in the Body of the Lord?" (*1 Cor* 10:16).

14. A third movement, which can be more brief and also function as a conclusion, suggests how the members of the community, transformed by the Eucharist, can carry the Gospel into the world in their daily lives. Naturally, the scriptural readings will provide the content and direction for such applications, but the homilist also needs to highlight the effect of the Eucharist itself, soon to be celebrated, and its consequences for daily living in the blessed hope of inseparable communion with God.

15. In sum, the homily is shaped by a very simple dynamic: it reflects on the meaning of the readings and prayers of a given celebration in light of the Paschal Mystery; and it leads the assembly to the Eucharistic celebration in which they have communion in the Paschal Mystery itself. (Examples of this approach to preaching will be given in Part Two of the *Directory*.) Clearly, this means that the liturgical setting is an essential key to interpreting the biblical passages proclaimed in a celebration, and it is to that interpretation that we now turn.

II. INTERPRETING THE WORD OF GOD IN THE LITURGY

16. The post-conciliar liturgical reform has enabled preaching on a richer collection of biblical readings during Mass. But what to say about them? In practice, the homilist often answers this question by consulting biblical commentaries to give some background on the readings, and then offers some kind of general moral application. What is sometimes lacking is sensitivity to the unique nature of the homily as an integral part of the Eucharistic celebration. When the homily is understood to be an organic

part of the Mass, it becomes clear that the preacher is asked to see the constellation of the readings and prayers of the celebration as crucial to his interpretation of the Word of God. In the words of Pope Benedict XVI:

> The reform called for by the Second Vatican Council has borne fruit in a richer access to sacred Scripture, which is now offered in abundance, especially at Sunday Mass. The present structure of the Lectionary not only presents the more important texts of Scripture with some frequency, but also helps us to understand the unity of God's plan thanks to the interplay of the Old and New Testament readings, an interplay "in which Christ is the central figure, commemorated in his Paschal Mystery" [OLM 66] (VD 57).

The Lectionary which we now have is the result of a desire expressed at the Council that "the treasures of the bible are to be opened up more lavishly, so that richer fare may be provided for the faithful at the table of God's Word" (SC 51). But the Fathers of the Second Vatican Council not only bequeathed to us this Lectionary; they also provided sound principles for biblical exegesis which are particularly germane to the homily.

17. The *Catechism of the Catholic Church* presents the three criteria for interpreting Scripture enunciated by the Council in these words:

> 1. *Be especially attentive "to the content and unity of the whole Scripture".* Different as the books which compose it may be, Scripture is a unity by reason of the unity of God's plan, of which Christ Jesus is the centre and heart, open since his Passover.

>> The phrase "heart of Christ" can refer to Sacred Scripture, which makes known his heart, closed before the Passion, as the Scripture was obscure. But the Scripture has been opened since the Passion; since those who from then on have understood it, consider and discern in what way the prophecies must be interpreted (CCC 112, citing St Thomas Aquinas, *Expositio in Psalmos*, 21, 11).

> 2. *Read the Scripture within "the living Tradition of the whole Church".* According to a saying of the Fathers, Sacred Scripture is written principally in the Church's heart rather than in documents and records, for the Church carries in her Tradition the living memorial of God's Word, and it is the Holy Spirit who gives her the spiritual

interpretation of the Scripture ("... according to the spiritual meaning which the Spirit grants to the Church") (CCC 113, citing Origen, *Homiliae in Leviticum*, 5, 5).

3. *Be attentive to the analogy of faith.* By "analogy of faith" we mean the coherence of the truths of faith among themselves and within the whole plan of Revelation (CCC 114).

While these criteria are useful for interpreting Scripture in any context, they are especially helpful when it comes to preparing the homily for Mass. Let us consider each of them in turn in terms of their relationship to the homily.

18. First, "the content and unity of the whole Scripture". The beautiful passage from St Thomas Aquinas quoted in the *Catechism* underscores the relationship between the Paschal Mystery and the Scriptures. The Paschal Mystery opens the meaning of the Scriptures, "obscure" until that time (cf. *Lk* 24:26-27). Seen in this light, the preacher's office is to help his people read the Scriptures in the light of the Paschal Mystery in such a way that Christ can reveal his very heart to them, which for St Thomas coincides here with the content and centre of the Scriptures.

19. The unity of the whole Scripture is embodied in the very structure of the Lectionary by the way in which Scripture is spread out through the whole of the liturgical year. At its centre we find the Scriptures with which the Church proclaims and celebrates the Paschal Triduum. But this is prepared for by the Lenten lectionary and extended in the lectionary of the Easter Season. Something similar is seen in the Advent-Christmas-Epiphany cycles. And further, the unity of the whole Scripture is likewise embodied in the structure of the Sunday Lectionary or the Lectionary for Solemnities and major feasts. At the heart stands the Gospel passage for the day; the Old Testament reading is chosen in light of the Gospel, and the Responsorial Psalm is inspired by the reading that precedes it. The selection from the Apostle presents on Sundays a semi-continuous reading of Epistles, so it is not usually connected explicitly to the other readings. Nonetheless, precisely because of the unity of the whole Scripture, connections between the second reading can often be found with the Old Testament reading and the Gospel. Thus, the homilist is insistently invited

by the Lectionary to see the biblical readings as mutually revelatory, or, to use the words of the *Catechism* and *Dei Verbum* again, to see "the content and unity of the whole Scripture".

20. Second, "the living Tradition of the whole Church". In *Verbum Domini*, Pope Benedict XVI underscores a fundamental criterion of biblical hermeneutics: "*the primary setting for scriptural interpretation is the life of the Church*" (29). The relationship between Tradition and Scripture is profound and complex, but certainly the liturgy represents an important and unique manifestation of this relationship. An organic unity exists between the Bible and liturgy: over the long centuries during which the sacred Scriptures were being written and the biblical canon was taking shape, the People of God were gathering regularly to celebrate the liturgy; indeed, the writings were created in good part for such gatherings (cf. *Col* 4:16). The preacher must take account of these liturgical origins of the Scriptures and look to them for clues for how to open a text in the new context of the community to which he preaches, where the ancient text is still alive and ever new in the moment of its proclamation. Scripture, formed in the very context of liturgy, is already Tradition; Scripture, proclaimed and explained within the Eucharistic celebration of the Paschal Mystery is likewise Tradition. A tremendous treasure of interpretation has been accumulated through centuries of such liturgical celebration and proclamation in the life of the Church. The mystery of Christ is known and pondered ever more deeply by the Church, and the Church's knowledge of Christ *is* Tradition. And so the preacher is invited to approach the readings of a given celebration, not as an arbitrary selection of texts, but as an opportunity to reflect on the profound meaning of these biblical passages within the living Tradition of the whole Church, as that Tradition is expressed in the selected and combined readings and in the prayer texts of the liturgy. These prayer texts are themselves monuments of the Tradition and are organically connected to Scripture, either taken directly from the Word of God or inspired by it.

21. Third, "the analogy of faith". In a theological sense, this refers to the nexus of various doctrines and the hierarchy of the truths of the faith. The core of our faith is the mystery of the Trinity, and the invitation for us to participate in this divine life. This reality is revealed and effected through

the Paschal Mystery: hence the homilist must both interpret the Scriptures in such a way that the Paschal Mystery is proclaimed, and lead the people to enter into this mystery through the celebration of the Eucharist. This kind of interpretation has been an essential part of the apostolic preaching from the very earliest days of the Church, as we read in *Verbum Domini*:

> Here, at the heart, as it were, of the "Christology of the word", it is important to stress the unity of the divine plan in the incarnate Word: the New Testament thus presents the Paschal Mystery as being in accordance with the sacred Scriptures and as their deepest fulfillment. Saint Paul, in the *First Letter to the Corinthians*, states that Jesus Christ died for our sins "in accordance with the Scriptures" (15:3) and that he rose on the third day "in accordance with the Scriptures" (15:4). The Apostle thus relates the event of the Lord's death and resurrection to the history of the Old Covenant of God with his people. Indeed, he shows us that from that event history receives its inner logic and its true meaning. In the Paschal Mystery "the words of Scripture" are fulfilled; in other words, this death which took place "in accordance with the Scriptures" is an event containing a *logos*, an inner logic: the death of Christ testifies that the Word of God became thoroughly human "flesh", human "history". Similarly, the resurrection of Jesus takes place "on the third day in accordance with the Scriptures": since Jewish belief held that decay set in after the third day, the word of Scripture is fulfilled in Jesus who rises incorrupt. Thus Saint Paul, faithfully handing on the teaching of the Apostles (cf. *1 Cor* 15:3), stresses that Christ's victory over death took place through the creative power of the Word of God. This divine power brings hope and joy: this, in a word, is the liberating content of the paschal revelation. At Easter, God reveals himself and the power of the trinitarian love which shatters the baneful powers of evil and death (13).

It is this unity of the divine plan that makes it appropriate for the homilist to provide doctrinal and moral catechesis during the homily. Doctrinally, the divine and human natures of Christ united in a single person, the divinity of the Holy Spirit, the ontological capacity of the Spirit and the Son to unite us to the Father in sharing the life of the Holy Trinity, the divine nature of the Church in which these realities are known and shared in – these doctrines and more were formulated as the deepest sense of what the Scriptures proclaim and what the sacraments accomplish. In a homily such doctrines would not be presented as they might be in a learned treatise or in a scholarly explanation where the mysteries can be explored and pondered in depth. Nonetheless, such doctrines guide the preacher and ensure that he arrives at and preaches about the deepest meaning of Scripture and sacrament.

22. The Paschal Mystery, efficaciously encountered in the sacramental celebration, sheds light not only on the Scriptures that are proclaimed, but it also transforms the lives of those who hear them. So, a further purpose of the homily is to help God's people see how the Paschal Mystery shapes not only what we believe but it also enables us to act in the light of the realities we believe. The *Catechism*, through the words of St John Eudes, points out the identification with Christ, which is a fundamental condition of Christian living:

> I ask you to consider that our Lord Jesus Christ is your true head, and that you are one of his members. He belongs to you as the head belongs to its members; all that is his is yours: his spirit, his heart, his body and soul, and all his faculties. You must make use of all these as of your own, to serve, praise, love, and glorify God. You belong to him, as members belong to their head. and so he longs for you to use all that is in you, as if it were his own, for the service and glory of the Father (CCC 1698, citing St John Eudes, *Tractatus de admirabili corde Jesu*, 1, 5; cf. Office of Readings, August 19).

23. The *Catechism of the Catholic Church* is an invaluable resource for the preacher who would employ the three criteria for interpretation that we are discussing. It provides a remarkable example of "the unity of the whole Scripture," of "the living Tradition of the whole Church" and of "the analogy of faith." This becomes especially clear when the dynamic relationship of the *Catechism*'s four parts is appreciated. The *Catechism* presents what we believe, how we worship, how we live, and how we pray. These could be likened to four interrelated themes of a symphony. Pope St John Paul II pointed out this organic relationship in the Apostolic Constitution *Fidei depositum*:

The Liturgy itself is prayer; the confession of faith finds its proper place in the celebration of worship. Grace, the fruit of the sacraments, is the irreplaceable condition for Christian living, just as participation in the Church's liturgy requires faith. If faith is not expressed in works, it is dead (cf. *Jas* 2:14-16) and cannot bear fruit unto eternal life.

In reading the *Catechism of the Catholic Church* we can perceive the wondrous unity of the mystery of God, his saving will, as well as the central place of Jesus Christ, the only-begotten Son of God, sent by the Father, made man in the womb of the Blessed Virgin Mary by the power of the Holy Spirit, to be our Saviour. Having died and risen, Christ is always present in his Church, especially in the sacraments; he is the source of our faith, the model of Christian conduct and the Teacher of our prayer (2).

The marginal references that relate the four parts of the *Catechism* to one another provide a help to the preacher who, being attentive to the analogy of faith, seeks to interpret the word of God within the living Tradition of the Church and in the light of the unity of all Scripture. Likewise, the Scriptural index of the *Catechism* shows how saturated the Church's whole teaching is in the biblical Word, and this index could well be used by preachers to see how particular scriptural texts that may be the subject of their preaching are used in other contexts to put forward doctrine and moral teaching. Appendix I of the *Directory* provides a resource for the homilist in his use of the *Catechism*.

24. It should be clear from what has been said so far that while exegetical methods can be useful in homily preparation, it is also necessary for the preacher to be attentive to the spiritual sense of Scripture. The definition of this sense given by the Pontifical Biblical Commission suggests that this method of interpretation is particularly apt for the liturgy: "[The spiritual sense is] the meaning expressed by the biblical texts when read, under the influence of the Holy Spirit, in the context of the Paschal Mystery of Christ and of the new life which flows from it. This context truly exists. In it the New Testament recognises the fulfilment of the Scriptures. It is therefore quite acceptable to re-read the Scriptures in the light of this new context, which is that of life in the Spirit" (Pontifical Biblical Commission, *Interpretation of the Bible in the Church* II, B, 2,

cited in VD 37). Reading the Scriptures in this way is woven into the very fabric of Catholic life. A good example is the psalms we pray in the Liturgy of the Hours: whatever the literal circumstances that brought each psalm into being, we understand them in terms of the mystery of Christ and his Church, and they also give voice to the joys, sorrows, and even complaints that are part of our personal relationship with God.

25. The great masters of the spiritual interpretation of Scripture are the Fathers of the Church, who were for the most part pastors, and whose writings often represent their explanations of the Word of God given to the people during the liturgy. It is providential that, along with the advances in biblical scholarship over the past century, there has been a corresponding advance in patristic studies as well. Lost documents have been discovered, critical editions of the Fathers have been produced, and great works of patristic and medieval exegesis are now available in translation. The revision of the Office of Readings in the Liturgy of the Hours has made many of these writings available to preachers and people alike. Familiarity with the writings of the Fathers can greatly aid the homilist in discovering the spiritual meaning of Scripture. It is from the Fathers' preaching that we learn how profound is the unity between Old Testament and New. From them we can learn to detect innumerable figures and patterns of the Paschal Mystery that are present in the world from the dawn of creation and that further unfold throughout the history of Israel that culminates in Jesus Christ. It is from the Fathers that we learn that virtually every word of the inspired Scriptures can yield unexpected and unfathomable riches when pondered in the heart of the Church's life and prayer. It is from the Fathers that we learn how intimately connected is the mystery of the biblical Word to the mystery of the sacramental celebration. The *Catena Aurea* of St Thomas Aquinas remains a splendid tool for accessing the riches of the Fathers. The Second Vatican Council clearly recognised that patristic writings represent a rich resource for the preacher:

> Priests are admonished by their bishop in the sacred rite of ordination that they "be mature in knowledge" and that their doctrine be "spiritual medicine for the People of God". The knowledge of the sacred minister ought to be sacred because it is drawn from the sacred source and directed to a sacred goal. Especially is it drawn from reading and

meditating on the Sacred Scriptures, and it is equally nourished by the study of the Holy Fathers and other Doctors and monuments of tradition (*Presbyterorum Ordinis* 19).

The Council has bequeathed to us a renewed understanding of the homily as integral to the liturgical celebration, a fruitful method for biblical interpretation, and an incentive for preachers to familiarise themselves with the riches of two thousand years of reflection on the Word of God that is the Catholic patrimony. How can a preacher realise this vision in practice?

III. PREPARATION

26. "Preparation for preaching is so important a task that a prolonged time of study, prayer, reflection and pastoral creativity should be devoted to it" (EG 145). Pope Francis emphasises this admonition with very strong words: a preacher who does not prepare himself and who does not pray is "dishonest and irresponsible" (EG 145), "a false prophet, a fraud, a shallow impostor" (EG 151). Clearly, in the preparation of homilies, study is invaluable, but prayer is essential. The homily will be delivered in a context of prayer, and it should be composed in a context of prayer. "The one presiding at the liturgy of the word communicates the spiritual nourishment it contains to those present, especially in the homily" (OLM 38). The sacred action of preaching is intimately joined to the sacred nature of the Word of God. The homily in some sense parallels the distribution of the Lord's Body and Blood to the faithful during the communion rite. In the homily God's holy Word is "distributed" for the nourishment of his people. The *Dogmatic Constitution on Divine Revelation* cautions the homilist, in the words of St Augustine, to avoid being "an empty preacher of the word of God outwardly, who is not a listener to it inwardly"; and further on in the same paragraph all Catholics are exhorted to read Scripture as a prayerful conversation with God for, according to St Ambrose, "We speak to him when we pray; we hear him when we read the divine saying" (DV 25). Pope Francis emphasises that preachers must allow themselves to be pierced by the living and active Word of God if it is to penetrate into the hearts of their hearers (cf. EG 150).

27. The Holy Father recommends that preachers seeking this profound dialogue with the Word of God have recourse to *lectio divina*, which consists of reading, meditation, prayer, and contemplation (cf. EG 152). This fourfold approach is rooted in the patristic exegesis of the spiritual senses of Scripture and was developed in subsequent centuries by monks and nuns who prayerfully pondered the Scriptures throughout a lifetime. Pope Benedict XVI describes the stages of *lectio divina* in his Apostolic Exhortation *Verbum Domini*:

> It opens with the reading (*lectio*) of a text, which leads to a desire to understand its true content: *what does the biblical text say in itself?* Without this, there is always a risk that the text will become a pretext for never moving beyond our own ideas. Next comes meditation (*meditatio*), which asks: *what does the biblical text say to us?* Here, each person, individually but also as a member of the community, must let himself or herself be moved and challenged. Following this comes prayer (*oratio*), which asks the question: *what do we say to the Lord in response to his Word?* Prayer, as petition, intercession, thanksgiving and praise, is the primary way by which the word transforms us. Finally, *lectio divina* concludes with contemplation (*contemplatio*), during which we take up, as a gift from God, his own way of seeing and judging reality, and ask ourselves *what conversion of mind, heart and life is the Lord asking of us?* In the *Letter to the Romans*, Saint Paul tells us: "Do not be conformed to this world, but be transformed by the renewal of your mind, that you may prove what is the will of God, what is good and acceptable and perfect" (*Rom* 12:2). Contemplation aims at creating within us a truly wise and discerning vision of reality, as God sees it, and at forming within us "the mind of Christ" (*1 Cor* 2:16). The word of God appears here as a criterion for discernment: it is "living and active, sharper than any two-edged sword, piercing to the division of soul and spirit, of joints and marrow, and discerning the thoughts and intentions of the heart" (*Heb* 4:12). We do well also to remember that the process of *lectio divina* is not concluded until it arrives at action (*actio*), which moves the believer to make his or her life a gift for others in charity (VD 87).

28. This is a very fruitful way for all people to pray with the Scriptures, and it recommends itself to the preacher as a way to meditate on the biblical readings and liturgical texts in a prayerful spirit when preparing his homily. The dynamic of *lectio divina* also offers a fruitful paradigm for an understanding of the role of the homily in the liturgy and how this affects the process of preparation.

29. The first step is *lectio*, which explores what the biblical text says in itself. This prayerful reading should be marked by an attitude of humble and awe-filled veneration of the word, which is expressed by taking time to study it with the greatest care and a holy fear lest the preacher distort it (cf. EG 146). As a preparation for this first step, the homilist should consult commentaries, dictionaries, and other scholarly resources that can help him understand what the biblical passages meant in their original context. But then he must also observe carefully the *incipit* and *explicit* of the passages in question in order to determine the significance of why the Lectionary begins and ends them where it does. Pope Benedict XVI teaches that historical-critical exegesis is an indispensible part of the Catholic understanding of Scripture because it is linked to the realism of the Incarnation. He says, "The historical fact is a constitutive dimension of the Christian faith. The history of salvation is not mythology, but a true history, and it should thus be studied with the methods of serious historical research" (VD 32). This first step should not be passed over too quickly. Our salvation is accomplished by the action of God in history, and the biblical text recounts this action in words that reveal the deepest sense of this action (cf. DV 3). So, we need this testimony of events, and the preacher needs a strong sense of their reality. "The Word became flesh," or "The Word became history," we might say. The practice of *lectio* begins by taking into account this awesome fact.

30. Some biblical scholars have not only written biblical commentaries, but also reflections on the readings in the Lectionary that apply the tools of modern scholarship to the texts proclaimed at Mass; such books can be of great help to the preacher. As he begins *lectio divina*, the homilist can review the insights he has gained from study, and prayerfully reflect on the meaning the biblical text. He should bear in mind, however, that

his aim is not to understand every little detail of a text, but to discover its principal message, the message which gives structure and unity to the text (cf. EG 147).

31. Because the aim of this *lectio* is to prepare a homily, the preacher must take care to translate the results of his study into language that can be understood by his hearers. Citing the teaching of Pope Paul VI that people will greatly benefit from preaching that is "simple, clear, direct, well-adapted" (*Evangelii Nuntiandi* 43), Pope Francis warns preachers against using specialised theological language which is unfamiliar to his hearers (cf. EG 158). He also offers some very practical advice:

> One of the most important things is to learn how to use images in preaching, how to appeal to imagery. Sometimes examples are used to clarify a certain point, but these examples usually appeal only to the mind; images, on the other hand, help people better to appreciate and accept the message we wish to communicate. An attractive image makes the message seem familiar, close to home, practical and related to everyday life. A successful image can make people savour the message, awaken a desire and move the will towards the Gospel (EG 157).

32. The second step, *meditatio*, explores what the biblical text says to us. Pope Francis suggests a few simple but penetrating questions that can shape our meditation: "Lord, what does this text say *to me*? What is it about my life that you want me to change by this text? What troubles me about this text? What do I find pleasant in this text? What is it about this word that moves me? What attracts me? Why does it attract me?" (EG 153). But the tradition of *lectio* tells us that this does not mean that by our own reflections we are the final arbiters of what the text is saying. In determining "what the text says to us" we are guided by the Church's Rule of Faith, which provides an essential principle of biblical interpretation that helps safeguard against erroneous or partial interpretations (cf. EG 148). So here the homilist reflects on the readings in light of the Paschal Mystery of Christ's death and Resurrection, and he extends his meditation to this mystery as it is lived out within Christ's Body, the Church, including the circumstances of the members of the Body that will gather on Sunday. This is the heart of the homiletic preparation itself. It is here that familiarity

with the writings of the Fathers of the Church and the saints can inspire the preacher to provide his people with an understanding of the readings at Mass that will truly nourish their spiritual lives. It is also at this stage of preparation that he can explore the doctrinal and moral implications of the Word of God, for which, as has been noted, the *Catechism of the Catholic Church* is a useful resource.

33. Along with reading the Scriptures within the context of the whole Tradition of the Catholic faith, the homilist also needs to reflect on it within the context of the community who will gather to listen to the Word of God. In the words of Pope Francis, "The preacher also needs to keep his ear to the people and to discover what it is that the faithful need to hear. A preacher has to contemplate the Word, but he also has to contemplate his people" (EG 154). This is one reason why it is helpful to begin preparing the Sunday homily several days before it is to be delivered: along with study and prayer, attention to what is happening in the parish and the wider society will suggest avenues of reflection about what the Word of God has to say to this community at this moment. Discerning again and again the pattern of Christ's death and resurrection in the life of the community and the world will be the fruit of such meditation. It will strongly shape the content of the homily.

34. The third stage of *lectio* is *oratio*, which answers the Lord in response to his Word. In the individual's experience of *lectio*, this is a time for unscripted conversation with God. Reactions to the readings are expressed in words of awe and wonder, or one is moved to ask for mercy and help, or, again, there might be a simple outburst of praise, expressions of love and gratitude. This shift from meditation to prayer, when considered in the context of the liturgy, highlights the organic connection between the biblical readings and the rest of the Mass. The intercessions that conclude the Liturgy of the Word, and more profoundly the Liturgy of the Eucharist that follows, represent our response to God's Word in petition, intercession, thanksgiving and praise. The homilist should on occasion explicitly underscore this integral relationship, so that God's people come to experience more deeply the inner dynamic of the liturgy.

This connection can also be reinforced in other ways. The preacher's role is not limited to the homily itself: the petitions offered during the Penitential Rite (if the third form is used) and the intercessions in the Universal Prayer can allude to the readings or a point made in the homily; the Entrance and Communion Antiphons prescribed by the *Roman Missal* for each celebration are almost always Scriptural texts or strongly based on them and so give voice to our prayer in the very words of the Scriptures. Or if these cannot be used, then hymns should also be chosen carefully, and the priest should guide those involved with the ministry of music in this regard. There is another way the priest can underscore the unity of the liturgical celebration, through a judicious use of the opportunities provided by the *General Instruction of the Roman Missal* for brief comments at various points in the liturgy: after the greeting, before the Liturgy of the Word, before the Eucharistic Prayer, and before the dismissal (cf. 31). Great care and restraint should be exercised in this regard. *There should be only one homily at Mass.* If the priest chooses to say something at any of these points, he should prepare in advance a succinct sentence or two that helps the people sense the unity of the liturgical celebration without going into an exhaustive explanation.

35. The final stage of *lectio* is *contemplatio*, during which, in the words of Pope Benedict XVI, "we take up, as a gift from God, his own way of seeing and judging reality, and ask ourselves *what conversion of mind, heart and life is the Lord asking of us?*" (VD 87). In the monastic tradition this fourth stage, contemplation, was seen as the gift of union with God – undeserved, greater than our efforts could ever achieve, sheer gift. A particular text had begun the process, but this point of arrival had moved beyond particulars to a grasp in faith of the whole in a single, intuitive and unitive glance. The saints show us these heights, but what is given to the saints can belong to us all.

When this fourth stage of contemplation is considered in the liturgical setting, it can be a consolation to the preacher and give him hope, because it is a reminder that it is ultimately God who is at work bringing his Word to fruition, and that the process of forming the mind of Christ within us takes place over a lifetime. The homilist should make every effort to preach God's Word effectively, but in the end, as St Paul said, "I planted, Apollos watered, but God gave the growth" (*1 Cor* 3:6). The homilist ought to pray to the Holy Spirit for enlightenment while preparing his homily, but he should also pray often and insistently that the seed of God's Word will fall on good ground and sanctify him and his hearers in ways that far exceed what he manages to say or even imagines.

36. Pope Benedict XVI added a coda to the traditional fourfold process of *lectio divina*: "We do well also to remember that the process of *lectio divina* is not concluded until it arrives at action (*actio*), which moves the believer to make his or her life a gift for others in charity" (VD 87). Viewed in its liturgical context, this suggests the "*missa*", the sending out of God's people who have been instructed by God's Word and nourished by their participation in the Paschal Mystery through the Eucharist. It is significant that the Exhortation *Verbum Domini* concludes with a lengthy consideration of the Word of God in the world; preaching, when combined with the nourishment of the sacraments received in faith, opens up the members of the liturgical assembly to practical expressions of charity. Similarly, citing Pope St John Paul II's teaching that "communion and mission are profoundly interconnected" (*Christifideles Laici* 32), Pope Francis exhorts all believers:

> In fidelity to the example of the Master, it is vitally important for the Church today to go forth and preach the Gospel to all: to all places, on all occasions, without hesitation, reluctance or fear. The joy of the Gospel is for all people: no one can be excluded (EG 23).

PART TWO:

ARS PRAEDICANDI

37. When describing the task of preaching, Pope Francis teaches: "The heart of its message will always be the same: the God who revealed his immense love in the crucified and risen Christ" (EG 11). The purpose of this section of the *Homiletic Directory* is to provide concrete examples and suggestions to help the homilist put into practice the principles presented in this document by considering the biblical readings provided in the liturgy through the lens of the Paschal Mystery of the crucified and risen Christ. These are not sample homilies, but sketches that propose ways of approaching particular themes and texts throughout the course of the liturgical year. The *Introduction of the Lectionary* provides brief descriptions of the choice of readings "to assist pastors of souls to understand the structure of the Order of Readings, so that their use of it will become more perceptive and the Order of Readings a source of good for Christ's faithful" (OLM 92). These will be cited. In all that is proposed concerning any of the texts of Scripture, it should always be borne in mind that "The reading of the Gospel is the high point of the liturgy of the word. For this the other readings, in their established sequence from the Old to the New Testament, prepare the assembly" (OLM 13).

38. The starting point of the presentation here is the Lectionary of the Paschal Triduum, for this is the centre of the liturgical year, and some of the most important passages from both Testaments are proclaimed during the course of these most holy days. This is followed by reflections on the Easter Season and Pentecost. Next, the readings of the Sundays of Lent will be considered. Further examples are taken from the Advent-Christmas-Epiphany cycle. This plan of proceeding follows what Pope Benedict XVI has called "the sage pedagogy of the Church, which proclaims and listens to sacred Scripture following the rhythm of the liturgical year." And he continues, "At the centre of everything the Paschal Mystery shines forth, and around it radiate all the mysteries of Christ and the history of salvation which become sacramentally present..." (VD 52).

So, in what is offered here, no attempt is made to exhaust all that could be said about a given celebration or to move in detail through the whole liturgical year. Rather, in the light of the centrality of the Paschal Mystery, indications are offered on how particular texts could be handled within a given homily. The pattern suggested by these examples can be adapted for the Sundays in Ordinary Time and other occasions. The pattern would be valid, and so useful, also for those other rites of the Catholic Church that use a different Lectionary from the Roman rite.

I. THE PASCHAL TRIDUUM AND THE FIFTY DAYS

A. *The Old Testament Reading on Holy Thursday*

39. "On Holy Thursday at the evening Mass the remembrance of the meal preceding the Exodus casts its own special light because of the Christ's example in washing the feet of his disciples and Paul's account of the institution of the Christian Passover in the Eucharist" (OLM 99). The Paschal Triduum begins with the Evening Mass, where the liturgy remembers the Lord's institution of the Eucharist. Jesus entered into his Passion by celebrating the meal prescribed in the first reading: its every word and image point to what Christ himself pointed to at table, his life-giving death. The words from the Book of Exodus (*Ex* 12:1-8, 11-14) find their definitive meaning in Jesus's paschal meal, the same meal we are celebrating now.

40. "Every family shall join the nearest household in procuring a lamb." We are many households come together in one place, and we have procured a lamb. "The lamb must be a year-old male and without blemish." Our unblemished lamb is no less than Jesus himself, the Lamb of God. "With the whole assembly of Israel present, the lamb shall be slaughtered during the evening twilight." As we hear those words, we grasp that we are the whole assembly of the new Israel, gathered in the evening twilight; Jesus lets himself be slaughtered as he hands over his body and blood for us. "They shall apply the lamb's blood to the doorposts and lintels … and that same night eat its roasted flesh." We shall fulfil these prescriptions as we take the blood of Jesus, applying it to our lips and eat the flesh of the Lamb in the consecrated bread.

41. We are told to eat this meal "with your loins girt, sandals on your feet and your staff in hand, like those who are in flight". This is a description of our Christian life in the world. The girt loins suggest readiness to flee, but also evoke the scene of the *mandatum* that is described in tonight's Gospel and takes place after the homily: we are called to be of service to the world, but as those who are sojourning, whose true home is not here. It is at this point in the reading, when we are told to eat like those in flight that the Lord solemnly names the feast: "It is the Passover (in Hebrew *pesach*) of the Lord! For on this same night I will strike down the first-born in the land ... but, seeing the blood, I will pass over you." The Lord fights for us to strike down our enemies, sin and death, and protects us through the blood of the Lamb.

42. This solemn announcement of the Pasch concludes with a final order: "This day shall be a memorial feast for you ... a perpetual institution." Not only did faithfulness to this command keep the Pasch alive in every generation down to the time of Jesus and beyond, but our faithfulness to his command, "Do this in memory of me" brings every subsequent generation of Christians into communion with Jesus's Pasch. This is precisely what we do at this moment as we begin this year's Triduum. It is a "memorial feast" instituted by the Lord, a "perpetual institution," a liturgical re-enacting of Jesus's total gift of self.

B. The Old Testament Reading on Good Friday

43. "On Good Friday the liturgical service has as its centre John's narrative of the Passion of him who was proclaimed in Isaiah as the Servant of the Lord and who became the one High Priest by offering himself to the Father" (OLM 99). The selection from Isaiah (*Is* 52:13-53:12) is one of the passages from the Old Testament in which Christians first saw the prophets pointing to the death of Christ. In relating this passage to the Passion, we follow a very ancient apostolic tradition, for this is what Philip did in his conversation with the Ethiopian eunuch (cf. *Acts* 8:26-40).

44. The assembly is well aware of the reason for today's gathering: to remember the death of Jesus. The prophet's words comment, as it were, from God's point of view on the scene of Jesus hanging on the Cross. We

are invited to see the glory hidden in the Cross: "See, my servant shall prosper, he shall be raised high and greatly exalted." Jesus himself, in John's Gospel spoke on several occasions of being lifted up; it is clear in this Gospel that there are three intertwined dimensions to this "lifting up": on the Cross, in his Resurrection, and in his Ascension to his Father.

45. But immediately after this glorious beginning to the Father's "comment", its counterpoint is pronounced: the agony of the crucifixion. The servant is described as one "whose look was marred beyond human semblance and his appearance beyond that of the sons of man". In Jesus, the Eternal Word has not only assumed our human flesh, but embraces death in its most hideous and dehumanizing form. "So shall he startle many nations, because of him kings shall stand speechless." These words describe the history of the world from that first Good Friday to today: the story of the Cross has startled nations and converted them, it has startled others and caused them to turn away. The prophetic words apply to our community and culture as well, and to the host of "nations" within each of us – our energies and tendencies which must be converted to the Lord.

46. What follows is no longer God's voice, but the prophet's: "Who would believe what we have heard?" He then proceeds with a description whose details lead us to a further contemplation of the Cross, a contemplation that interlaces passion and passage, suffering and glory. The depth of suffering is further described with an exactness that makes us understand how natural it was for the first Christians to read texts of this kind and understand them as a prophetic foreshadowing of Christ, perceiving the glory hidden within. And thus, as the prophet claims, this tragic figure is full of significance for us: "Yet it was our infirmities that he bore, our sufferings that he endured … by his stripes we were healed."

47. Jesus's own interior attitude to his Passion is also foretold: "Though he was harshly treated, he submitted … like a lamb led to the slaughter … he was silent and opened not his mouth…." These are all startling and amazing things. But in effect the Resurrection is obliquely foretold as well in what the prophet says: "If he gives his life as an offering for sin, he shall see his descendants in a long life." All believers are those descendants; his "long life" is the eternal life the Father gives him in

"Novels...
teach you
the secret,
that the
best of life is
conversation."
—*Ralph Waldo
Emerson*

raising him from the dead. And now the Father's voice is heard again, continuing to proclaim the promise of Resurrection: "Because of his affliction he shall see the light in fulness of days... Therefore I will give him his portion among the great, and he shall divide the spoils with the mighty, because he surrendered himself to death... he shall take away the sins of many, and win pardon for their offences."

C. The Old Testament Readings of the Easter Vigil

48. "At the Vigil on the holy night of Easter there are seven Old Testament readings which recall the wonderful works of God in the history of salvation. There are two New Testament readings, the announcement of the Resurrection according to one of the Synoptic Gospels and a reading from St Paul on Christian baptism as the sacrament of Christ's Resurrection" (OLM 99). The Easter Vigil is, as the *Roman Missal* indicates, "the greatest and most noble of all solemnities" (Easter Vigil 2). The length of the Vigil does not allow for extended commentary on the seven readings from the Old Testament, but it should be noted that they are central, representative texts proclaiming whole blocks of essential Old Testament theology, moving from creation through Abraham's sacrifice to the most important reading, the Exodus; four subsequent readings announce pivotal themes of the prophets. An understanding of these texts in relation to the Paschal Mystery, which is so explicit in the Easter Vigil, can inspire the homilist when these or similar readings appear at other times in the liturgical year.

49. In the context of the liturgy of this night, the Church progresses by way of these lessons to the climax of them all, the Gospel account of the Lord's Resurrection. We are plunged into the stream of salvation history by means of the Sacraments of Initiation, celebrated on this evening, as Paul's beautiful passage on Baptism reminds us. The links which are so clear in this night between creation and the new life in Christ, between the historical Exodus and the definitive Exodus of Jesus's Paschal Mystery in which all the faithful share through Baptism, between the prophets' promises and their realisation in the very liturgies being celebrated – all these are links that can be made again and again throughout the liturgical year.

50. A very rich resource for understanding these links between Old Testament themes and their fulfilment in Christ's Paschal Mystery is the prayers that follow each reading. These express with simplicity and clarity the Church's profound Christological and sacramental understanding of the Old Testament texts, as they speak of creation, sacrifice, the exodus, baptism, divine mercy, the eternal covenant, the cleansing of sin, redemption and life in Christ. They can serve as a school of prayer for the homilist not only as he prepares for the Easter Vigil, but also throughout the year when treating texts similar to those proclaimed this evening. Another useful resource for interpreting the Scripture passages is the responsorial psalm that follows each of the seven readings, the poems sung by Christians who have died with Christ and now share with him in his risen life. These should not be neglected through the rest of the year, for they demonstrate how the Church reads all Scripture in the light of Christ.

D. The Easter Lectionary

51. "The Gospel reading for the Mass on Easter day is from John on the finding of the empty tomb. There is also, however, the option to use the Gospel texts from the Easter Vigil or, when there is an evening Mass on Easter Sunday, to use the account in Luke of the Lord's appearance to the disciples on the road to Emmaus. The first reading is from the Acts of the Apostles, which throughout the Easter season replaces the Old Testament reading. The reading from the Apostle Paul concerns the living out of the Paschal Mystery in the Church. ... The Gospel readings for the first three Sundays recount the appearances of the risen Christ. The readings about the Good Shepherd are assigned to the Fourth Sunday. On the Fifth, Sixth, and Seventh Sundays, there are excerpts from the Lord's discourse and prayer at the end of the Last Supper" (OLM 99-100). Following upon the rich collection of readings from the Old and New Testaments heard during the Triduum, these are some of the most intense moments of the proclamation of the risen Lord in the life of the Church, and they are meant to be instructive and formative of the People of God throughout the whole liturgical year. During Holy Week and the Easter Season, the homilist will have occasion again and again to drive home the point, based

on the scriptural texts themselves, of the Passion, Death, and Resurrection of Christ as the central content of the Scriptures. This is the privileged liturgical season during which the homilist can and must put forward the Church's faith on this, her central proclamation: that Jesus Christ died for our sins "in accordance with the Scriptures" (*1 Cor* 15:3) and that he rose on the third day "in accordance with the Scriptures" (*1 Cor* 15:4).

52. First, there is an opportunity, especially on the first three Sundays, to impart various dimensions of the Church's *lex credendi* in this privileged season. The paragraphs of the *Catechism of the Catholic Church* that treat the resurrection (CCC 638-658) are, in fact, an unfolding of many of the key biblical texts that are proclaimed during the Easter season. These paragraphs can be a sure guide to the homilist who should explain to the Christian people, on the basis of the scriptural texts, what the *Catechism* calls in turn, in various of its headings "The Historical and Transcendent Event" of the resurrection, the significance of "the appearances of the Risen One," "The condition of Christ's risen humanity," and "The Resurrection – a Work of the Holy Trinity."

53. Second, during the Sundays of Easter the first reading is taken, not from the Old Testament, but from the Acts of the Apostles. Many of the passages are examples of the earliest apostolic preaching, and we see in them how the apostles themselves used the Scriptures to announce the significance of the death and resurrection of Jesus. In other passages, the consequences of Jesus's resurrection and its effects in the life of the Christian community are recounted. From these passages, the homilist has in hand some of his strongest and most basic tools. He sees how the apostles used the Scriptures to announce the death and resurrection of Jesus, and he does the same, not only in the passage at hand but in this same style throughout the whole of the liturgical year. He also sees the power of the life of the risen Lord at work in the first communities, and he declares in faith to his own people that the same power is still at work among us.

54. Third, the intensity of Holy Week itself, with its Paschal Triduum, followed by the joyful celebration of fifty days that climax in Pentecost, is an excellent time for the homilist to draw links between the Scriptures

and the Eucharist. It was precisely in the "breaking of the bread" – which recalled Jesus's total gift of self at the Last Supper and then upon the Cross – that the disciples realised that their hearts burned within them as the risen Lord opened their minds to the understanding of the Scriptures. A similar pattern of understanding is to be hoped for still today. The homilist works diligently to explain the Scriptures, but the deeper meaning of what he says will emerge in "the breaking of the bread" at that same liturgy if the homilist has built bridges to that moment (cf. VD 54). The importance of such bridges is forcefully stated by Pope Benedict in *Verbum Domini*:

> From these accounts [of resurrection] it is clear that Scripture itself points us towards an appreciation of its own unbreakable bond with the Eucharist. "It can never be forgotten that the divine word, read and proclaimed by the Church, has as its one purpose the sacrifice of the new covenant and the banquet of grace, that is, the Eucharist." Word and Eucharist are so deeply bound together that we cannot understand one without the other: the Word of God sacramentally takes flesh in the event of the Eucharist. The Eucharist opens us to an understanding of Scripture, just as Scripture for its part illumines and explains the mystery of the Eucharist (55).

55. Fourth, from the Fifth Sunday of Easter on, the dynamic of the readings shifts from celebration of the Lord's Resurrection to preparation for the culmination of the Paschal Season, the coming of the Holy Spirit at Pentecost. The fact that the Gospel readings on these Sundays are all taken from Christ's discourse at the end of the Last Supper underscores their profoundly eucharistic significance. The readings and prayers provide an opportunity for the homilist to treat the role of the Holy Spirit in the ongoing life of the Church. The paragraphs of the *Catechism* that treat of "God's Spirit and Word in the Time of the Promises" (CCC 702-716) offer a reprise of the readings from the Easter Vigil, seen now in terms of the work of the Holy Spirit, and those dealing with "The Holy Spirit and the Church in the Liturgy" (CCC 1091-1109) can assist the homilist to speak about how the Holy Spirit makes present the Paschal Mystery of Christ in the liturgy.

56. With preaching that embodies these principles and points of view throughout the Easter Season, the Christian People is well prepared for

the celebration of the Solemnity of Pentecost, where God the Father "through his Word, pours into our hearts the Gift that contains all gifts, the Holy Spirit" (CCC 1082). The reading from Acts on that day recounts the Pentecost event itself, while the Gospel gives an account of what happened on the evening of Easter Sunday itself. The risen Lord breathed on his disciples and said, "Receive the Holy Spirit" (*Jn* 20:22). Easter *is* Pentecost. Easter is already the gift of the Holy Spirit. But Pentecost is the convincing manifestation of Easter to all the nations, uniting many tongues in one new language of understanding "the mighty acts of God" (*Acts* 2:11) displayed in Jesus's death and resurrection. As the Church moves into the Eucharistic prayer on that day, she prays that "the Holy Spirit may reveal to us more abundantly the hidden mystery of this sacrifice and graciously lead us into all truth" (Prayer over the Offerings). The reception of Holy Communion by the faithful on that day becomes the Pentecost event for them. While they come forward in procession to receive the Lord's Body and Blood, the Communion Antiphon places in song on their tongues the scriptural verses of the Pentecost account that say, "They were all filled with the Holy Spirit and spoke of the marvels of God, alleluia." The scriptural verses find their fulfilment in the faithful receiving the Eucharist. Eucharist *is* Pentecost.

II. THE SUNDAYS OF LENT

57. If the Paschal Triduum and the Fifty Days are the radiant centre of the liturgical year, Lent is the season that prepares the minds and hearts of the Christian people for a worthy celebration of these days. It is also the time for the final preparation of catechumens who will be baptised during the Easter Vigil. Their journey needs to be accompanied by the faith, prayer and witness of the entire ecclesial community. The scriptural readings of the Lenten season find their deepest sense in relation to the Paschal Mystery that they prepare us to celebrate. As such they provide clear occasions for putting into practice a fundamental principle that this *Directory* presents: to take the readings at Mass to their centre in Jesus's Paschal Mystery, into which Mystery we enter most deeply by the celebration of the paschal sacraments. The *Introduction of the Lectionary* notes the traditional use of accounts of the Temptation and Transfiguration

on the first two Sundays of Lent, and says this about the other readings: "The Old Testament readings are about the history of salvation, which is one of the themes proper to the catechesis of Lent. The series of texts for each Year presents the main elements of salvation history from its beginning until the promise of the New Covenant. The readings from the Letters of the Apostles have been selected to fit the Gospel and the Old Testament readings and, to the extent possible, to provide a connection between them" (OLM 97).

A. *The Gospel on the First Sunday of Lent*

58. It is not difficult for people to connect the forty days that Jesus passed in the desert with the forty days of Lent. It is useful for the homilist to draw this connection explicitly in such a way that the Christian people understand that the annual observance of Lent somehow makes them mysteriously participate in these forty days of Jesus, and in what he underwent and achieved in his fasting and being tempted. While it is customary for Catholics to engage in various penitential and devotional practices during this season, it is important to underscore the profoundly *sacramental* reality of the entire Lenten season. The Collect for the First Sunday of Lent uses the striking phrase "...*per annua quadragesimalis exercitia sacramenti*...". Christ himself is present and at work in his Church in this holy season, and it is his purifying work in the members of his Body that gives our penitential practices their salvific significance. The Preface assigned to this day states this idea beautifully when it says, "by abstaining forty long days from earthly food, he consecrated through his fast the pattern of our Lenten observance...". The language of the Preface is a bridge between Scripture and Eucharist.

59. The forty days of Jesus represent the forty years of Israel's wandering in the desert; the whole of Israel's history is concentrated in him. So here is a scene in which a major theme of this Directory is concentrated: the history of Israel, which corresponds to our life's history, finds its ultimate meaning in the Passion that Jesus undergoes. That Passion in some sense begins already here in the desert, virtually at the beginning of the public life of Jesus. So from the beginning, Jesus is moving toward his Passion, and everything that follows draws its meaning from this.

60. A paragraph taken from the *Catechism of the Catholic Church* can demonstrate its usefulness in preparing homilies, especially for touching on doctrinal themes that are directly rooted in the biblical text. About Jesus's temptations, the *Catechism* says

> The evangelists indicate the salvific meaning of this mysterious event: Jesus is the new Adam who remained faithful just where the first Adam had given in to temptation. Jesus fulfils Israel's vocation perfectly: in contrast to those who had once provoked God during forty years in the desert, Christ reveals himself as God's Servant, totally obedient to the divine will. In this, Jesus is the devil's conqueror.... Jesus's victory over the tempter in the desert anticipates victory at the Passion, the supreme act of obedience of his filial love for the Father (CCC 539).

61. The temptations that Jesus undergoes are a struggle against a distortion of his messianic task. The devil is tempting him to be a Messiah who displays divine powers. "If you are the Son of God..." the tempter begins. This foreshadows the ultimate struggle that Jesus will undergo on the cross, where he hears the mocking words: "Save yourself if you are the Son of God and come down from the cross." Jesus does not yield to the temptations of Satan, nor does he come down from the cross. Precisely in this way Jesus proves that he truly enters the desert of human existence and does not use his divine power for his own benefit. He really accompanies our life's pilgrimage and reveals in it the true power of God, which is love "to the very end" (*Jn* 13:1).

62. The homilist should point out that Jesus is subjected to temptation and death in solidarity with us. But the Good News that the homilist announces is not simply Jesus's solidarity with us in suffering; he also announces Jesus's victory over temptation and over death, a victory that Jesus shares with all who believe in him. The ultimate guarantee of Jesus sharing that victory with all who believe will be the celebration of the paschal sacraments at the Easter Vigil, toward which the first Sunday of Lent is already pointing. The homilist points in this same direction.

63. Jesus resisted the devil's temptation to turn stones into bread, but in the end and in ways the human mind could never have imagined, in his resurrection Jesus turns the "stone" of death into "bread" for us. Through

his death *he* becomes the bread of the Eucharist. The congregation that feeds on this heavenly bread might well be reminded by a homilist that the victory of Jesus over temptation and death in which they share through the sacraments turns their "hearts of stone into hearts of flesh," as the Lord promised through his prophet, hearts that strive to make God's merciful love tangible in their daily lives. Then Christian faith can act as a leaven in a world hungry for God, and stones are truly turned into the nourishment that fulfils the longing of the human heart.

B. The Gospel on the Second Sunday of Lent

64. The Gospel on the second Sunday of Lent is always the account of the Transfiguration. It is striking that the glorious and unexpected transfiguration of Jesus's body in the presence of three chosen disciples should take place immediately after his first prediction of his Passion. (These same three disciples – Peter, James, and John – will likewise be with Jesus during his agony in the garden as he enters into the very hour of his Passion.) In the context of the entire narrative of each of the three gospels, Peter has just confessed his faith in Jesus as Messiah. Jesus accepts this confession but immediately turns to teaching his disciples just what kind of Messiah he is. "He began to teach them that the Son of Man must suffer greatly and be rejected by the elders, the chief priests, and the scribes, and be killed, and rise after three days." Then he goes on to teach how the Messiah is to be followed: "Whoever wishes to come after me must deny himself, take up his cross and follow me." It is after this that Jesus takes three disciples up on a high mountain, and there divine glory bursts forth from his body. Moses and Elijah appear, and they are conversing with Jesus. Then a cloud of divine presence, like the one on Mount Sinai, envelops Jesus and his disciples, and from the cloud comes a voice, just as thunder on Sinai signalled that God was speaking to Moses and giving the Law, the Torah, to him. This is the voice of the Father, revealing the deepest identity of Jesus and accrediting him. He says, "This is my beloved Son. Listen to him" (*Mk* 9:7).

65. Many of the themes and patterns that this *Directory* has emphasised are concentrated in this stunning scene. Clearly, cross and glory belong together. Clearly, the whole Old Testament, represented in Moses and

Elijah, concurs that cross and glory belong together. The homilist must speak of these things and explain them. Perhaps no better summary could be found of what the mystery means than the beautiful words of the Preface assigned to that day. As the Eucharistic prayer begins, the priest, speaking for the whole people, wants to give thanks to God through Christ our Lord for this mystery of transfiguration: "For after he had told the disciples of his coming Death, on the holy mountain he manifested to them his glory, to show, even by the testimony of the law and the prophets, that the Passion leads to the glory of the Resurrection." These are the words with which the community begins the Eucharistic Prayer on this day.

66. In each of the Synoptic accounts, the Father's voice identifies Jesus as his beloved Son and commands, "Listen to him." In the midst of this scene of transcendent glory, the Father's command draws attention to the path to glory. It is as if he says, "Listen to him, in whom there is the fulness of my love, which will appear on the Cross." This teaching is a new Torah, the new Law of the Gospel, given on the holy mountain in the centre of which there is the grace of the Holy Spirit, given to those who place their faith in Jesus and in the merits of his Cross. It is because he teaches this way that glory bursts forth from Jesus's body and he is revealed as the Father's beloved Son. Are we not here deep inside the very heart of the trinitarian mystery? It is the Father's glory we see in the glory of the Son, and that glory is inextricably joined to the cross. The Son revealed in the transfiguration is "Light from Light," as the Creed states it; and surely this moment in the Sacred Scriptures is one of the strongest warrants for the Creed's formulation.

67. The Transfiguration holds an essential position in the season of Lent because the entire Lenten Lectionary is a lesson book that prepares the elect among the catechumens to receive the Sacraments of Initiation at the Easter Vigil, just as it prepares all the faithful to renew themselves in the new life into which they have been reborn. If the first Sunday of Lent is an especially striking reminder of Jesus's solidarity with us in temptation, the second Sunday is meant to remind us that the glory that bursts forth from Jesus's body is a glory that he means to share with all who are baptised into his death and resurrection. The homilist might well use the words and authority of St Paul to establish this point, who said,

"He [Christ] will change our lowly body to conform with his glorified body" (*Phil* 3:21). This verse is found in the second reading of Cycle C, but the short phrase can bring the point succinctly to the fore in any year.

68. As the faithful come in procession to communion on this Sunday, the Church has them sing in the Communion Antiphon the very words of the Father heard in the Gospel: "This is my beloved Son, with whom I am well pleased; listen to him." What the chosen three disciples heard and beheld at the transfiguration exactly converges now with the event of this liturgy in which the faithful receive the Body and Blood of the Lord. In the Prayer after Communion we thank God for allowing us while "still on earth" to be partakers of the things of heaven. While still on earth, the disciples saw the divine glory shining in the body of Jesus. While still on earth, the faithful receive his Body and Blood and hear the Father's voice speaking to them in the depths of their hearts: "This is my beloved Son, with whom I am well pleased; listen to him."

C. The Third, Fourth, and Fifth Sundays of Lent

69. "On the next three Sundays [of Lent], the Gospels about the Samaritan woman, the man born blind, and the raising of Lazarus have been restored in Year A. Because these Gospels are of major importance in regard to Christian initiation, they may also be read in Year B and Year C, especially in places where there are catechumens. Other texts, however, are provided for Year B and Year C: for Year B, a text from John about Christ's coming glorification through his Cross and Resurrection, and for Year C, a text from Luke about conversion. [...] Because the readings about the Samaritan woman, the man born blind, and the raising of Lazarus are now assigned to Sundays, but only for Year A (in Year B and Year C they are optional), provision has been made for their use on weekdays. Thus at the beginning of the Third, Fourth, and Fifth Weeks of Lent optional Masses with these texts for the Gospel have been inserted and may be used in place of the readings of the day on any weekday of the respective week" (OLM 97, 98). The catechetical power of the Lenten season is especially highlighted by the readings and prayers for the Sundays in Cycle A. The association of the themes of water, light, and life with baptism are quite evident; by means of these biblical passages and the prayers of the liturgy,

the Church is leading her elect toward sacramental initiation at Easter. Their final preparation is a fundamental concern, as the prayer texts used when the Scrutinies are celebrated make clear.

What of the rest of us? It may be helpful for the homilist to invite his listeners to view the Lenten season as a time for the reactivation of the graces of baptism and a purification of the faith that had been received. This process may be explained through the prism of Israel's understanding of the Exodus experience. That event was crucial to Israel's formation as the People of God, its discovery of its own limitations and unfaithfulness and also of the persistent and faithful love of God. Throughout Israel's subsequent history it served as a paradigm through which she could interpret her journey with God. So for us, Lent is a time when in the wilderness of our present existence with its difficulties, fears and infidelities we rediscover the proximity of God, who despite everything is leading us to our Promised Land. This is a fundamental moment in our life of faith that challenges us. The graces of baptism, received in infancy, are not to be forgotten, even though accumulated sin and human errors may suggest their absence. The desert is a place that tests our faith, but it also purifies it and strengthens it when we learn to base ourselves upon God in spite of contrary experiences. The underlying theme of these three Sundays is how faith can be nurtured continually even in the face of sin (the Samaritan woman), ignorance (the blind man), and death (Lazarus). These are the "deserts" through which we travel through life, and in which we discover that we are not alone, because God is with us.

70. The relationship between those preparing for baptism and the rest of the faithful enhances the dynamism of the Lenten season, and the homilist should make an effort to associate the wider community with the preparation of the elect. When the Scrutinies are celebrated, provision is made for a prayer for the godparents during the Eucharistic Prayer; this can serve as a reminder that each member of the congregation has a role to play in "sponsoring" the elect and bringing others to Christ. We who already believe are called, like the Samaritan woman, to share our faith with others. Then, at Easter, the newly-initiated can say to the rest of the community, "We no longer believe because of your word, for we have heard for ourselves, and know that he is truly the Saviour of the world."

71. The Third Sunday of Lent brings us back to the wilderness, with Jesus and Israel before him. The Israelites are thirsty, and their thirst causes them to question the wisdom of the journey God has launched them on. The situation seems hopeless, but help comes from a most surprising source: when Moses strikes the hard rock, water gushes forth! But there is a still harder, more obdurate substance – the human heart. The Responsorial Psalm makes an eloquent plea to those who sing and hear it: "If today you hear his voice, harden not your hearts." In the second reading, Paul tells us that the staff we wield is faith, which gives us access through Christ to the grace of God, and this in turn gives us hope. This hope does not disappoint, because the love of God has been poured into our hearts, enabling us to love. This divine love was given to us not as a reward for our merits, because it was given when we were still sinners, and yet Christ died for us. In just a few verses, the Apostle invites us to contemplate both the mystery of the Trinity and the virtues of faith, hope, and love.

The stage is set for the encounter between Jesus and the Samaritan woman, a conversation that is profound because it speaks of the fundamental realities of eternal life and true prayer. It is an illuminating conversation, because it manifests the pedagogy of faith. Jesus and the woman are initially talking on different levels. Her practical, concrete mind is centred on the water in the well. Jesus, as if oblivious of her practical concerns, insists on speaking about the living waters of grace. Since their discourses fail to meet, Jesus touches upon the most painful moment of her life: her irregular marital situation. This recognition of her frailty immediately opens her mind to the mystery of God, and she then asks about prayer. When she follows the invitation to believe in Jesus as the Messiah, she is filled with grace and is quick to share her discovery with those in her own town.

Faith, nourished by the Word of God, by the Eucharist and by the fulfilment of the will of the Father, opens to the mystery of grace that is depicted through the image of "living water". Moses struck the rock, and water flowed out; the soldier pierced the side of Christ, and blood and water flowed out. Mindful of this, the Church puts these words on the lips of the people as they process forward to receive Communion: "For anyone who drinks it, says the Lord, the water I shall give will become in him a spring welling up to eternal life."

72. But we are not the only ones who are thirsty. The Preface for today's Mass says: "When he asked the Samaritan woman for water to drink, he had already created the gift of faith within her and so ardently did he thirst for her faith, that he kindled in her the fire of divine love." The Jesus who sat down by the well was tired and thirsty. (In fact, the homilist may want to point out how the Gospels on these three Sundays underscore Christ's humanity: his exhaustion as he sat by the well, his making a mud with paste to heal the blind man, and his tears at the grave of Lazarus.) The thirst of Jesus will reach its climax in the final moments of his life, when from the Cross he cries out, "I thirst!" This is what it means for him to do the will of the one who sent him and to finish his work. Then from his pierced heart flows the eternal life that nourishes us in the sacraments, giving us who worship in spirit and in truth the nourishment we need as we continue our pilgrimage.

73. The Fourth Sunday of Lent is suffused with light, a light reflected on this "Laetare Sunday" by vestments of a lighter hue and the flowers that adorn the church. The association of the Paschal Mystery, baptism, and light is succinctly captured in a line from the second reading: "Awake, O sleeper, and arise from the dead, and Christ will give you light." This association finds an echo and an elaboration in the Preface: "By the mystery of the Incarnation, he has led the human race that walked in darkness into the radiance of faith and has brought those born in slavery to ancient sin through the waters of regeneration to make them your adopted children." This illumination, begun in baptism, is enhanced each time we receive the Eucharist, a point underscored by the words of the blind man taken up in the Communion Antiphon: "The Lord anointed my eyes: I went, I washed, I saw and believed in God."

74. But it is not a cloudless sky we contemplate on this Sunday; the process of seeing is in practice more difficult than the blind man's terse description. We are cautioned in the first reading: "Not as man sees does God see, because man sees the appearance but the Lord looks into the heart." This is a salutary warning both for the elect, whose anticipation grows as they draw near to Easter, and to the rest of the community as well. The Prayer after Communion states that God enlightens everyone who comes into the world: but the challenge is that, in great ways or small, we

turn toward the light or away from it. The homilist can invite his listeners to notice the increasing vision of the man born blind and the growing blindness of Jesus's adversaries. The cured man begins by describing his healer as "the man Jesus"; then he professes that he is a prophet; and by the end of the passage he proclaims, "I do believe, Lord" and worships Jesus. The Pharisees, for their part, become increasingly more blind: they begin by admitting that the miracle took place, then come to deny that it was a miracle, and finally expel the cured man from the synagogue. Throughout the narrative, the Pharisees continue to profess confidently what they know, while the blind man continually admits his ignorance. The Gospel ends with a warning by Jesus that his coming has created a crisis, in the literal meaning of that word, a judgement: he gives sight to the blind, but those who see become blind. In response to the Pharisees' objection, he says: "If you were blind, you would have no sin; but now you are saying, 'We see,' so your blindness remains." The illumination given in baptism must be tended amid the lights and shadows of our pilgrimage, and so after Communion we pray: "O God ... illuminate our hearts, we pray, with the splendour of your grace, that we may always ponder what is worthy and pleasing to your majesty and love you in all sincerity."

75. "Our friend Lazarus is asleep, but I am going to awaken him." Paul's exhortation to rouse the sleeper on the previous Sunday finds vivid expression in the last and greatest of Jesus's "signs" in the Fourth Gospel, the raising of Lazarus. The finality of death, emphasised by the fact that Lazarus had been already dead four days, seems to create an obstacle even greater than drawing water from a rock or giving sight to a man blind from birth. And yet, confronted with this state of affairs, Martha makes a profession of faith similar to Peter's: "I have come to believe that you are the Christ, the Son of God, the one who is coming into the world." Her faith is not in what God *could* do in the future, but to what God *is* doing now: "I am the resurrection and the life." This "I am" runs through John's Gospel, a clear allusion to the self-revelation of God to Moses, and it appears in the Gospels on each of these Sundays: when the Samaritan woman speaks about the Messiah, Jesus tells her, "I am he, the one speaking with you." In the story of the blind man, Jesus says, "While I am in the world, I am the light of the world." And today he says, "I am the resurrection and the life." The key to receiving this life is faith:

"Do you believe this?" But even Martha wavers after making her bold profession of faith, and objects when Jesus wants the stone to be removed that there will be a stench. Again, we are reminded that the following of Christ is the work of a lifetime, and whether we are about to receive the sacraments of initiation in two weeks time, or have lived many years as Catholics, we must struggle continually to deepen our faith in Christ.

76. The raising of Lazarus is the fulfilment of God's promise enunciated through the prophet Ezekiel in the first reading: "I will open your graves and have you rise from them." The heart of the Paschal Mystery is that Christ came to die and rise again precisely to do for us what he did for Lazarus: "Untie him and let him go." He frees us, not only from physical death, but from the many other deaths that afflict us and bind us: sin, misfortune, broken relationships. This is why it is essential for us as Christians to immerse ourselves continually in his Paschal Mystery. As the Preface today proclaims: "For as true man he wept for Lazarus his friend and as eternal God raised him from the tomb, just as, taking pity on the human race, he leads us by sacred mysteries to new life." Our weekly encounter with the crucified and risen Lord is the expression of our faith that he *IS*, here and now, our resurrection and our life. It is that conviction that enables us to accompany him next Sunday as he enters Jerusalem, saying with Thomas, "Let us also go and die with him."

D. Palm Sunday of the Lord's Passion

77. "On Palm Sunday of the Lord's Passion the texts for the procession are selections from the Synoptic Gospels concerning the Lord's solemn entry into Jerusalem. For the Mass the reading is the account of the Lord's Passion" (OLM 97). Two ancient traditions shape this unique liturgical celebration: the custom of a procession in Jerusalem, and the reading of the Passion in Rome. The exuberance surrounding Christ's regal entry immediately gives way to the reading of one of the Songs of the Suffering Servant and the solemn proclamation of the Lord's Passion. And this liturgy takes place on Sunday, a day *always* associated with the Resurrection of Christ. How can the preacher bring together the many theological and emotional elements of this day, especially since pastoral considerations suggest a rather short homily? The key is found in the second reading, the

beautiful hymn from St Paul's Letter to the Philippians, which admirably summarises the whole Paschal Mystery. The homilist could briefly point out that as the Church enters Holy Week, we will experience that Mystery in a way that speaks to our hearts. Various local customs and traditions draw people into the events of the final days of Jesus's life, but the great desire of the Church for this week is not simply to touch our emotions, but to deepen our faith. In the liturgical celebrations of the coming week we do not simply commemorate what Jesus did; we are plunged into the Paschal Mystery itself, dying and rising with Christ.

III. THE SUNDAYS OF ADVENT

78. "Each Gospel reading [for the Sundays in Advent] has a distinctive theme: the Lord's coming at the end of time (First Sunday of Advent), John the Baptist (Second and Third Sunday), and the events that prepared immediately for the Lord's birth (Fourth Sunday). The Old Testament readings are prophecies about the Messiah and the Messianic age, especially from the Book of Isaiah. The readings from an Apostle contain exhortations and proclamations, in keeping with the different themes of Advent" (OLM 93). Advent is the season that prepares the Christian people for the graces that will be given again this year in the celebration of the great solemnity of Christmas. From the First Sunday of Advent the homilist urges his people to undertake a preparation that has many facets, each suggested by the rich collection of scriptural passages in this part of the Lectionary. The first part of Advent season urges us to prepare for Christmas by encouraging us not only to look backward in time to our Lord's first coming when, as Preface I of Advent says, "he assumed the lowliness of human flesh," but also to look forward to his coming again "in glory and majesty," to a day when "all is at last made manifest."

79. So there is always this double sense of *adventus* – a double sense of the Lord's *coming*. The season prepares us for his coming in the graces of the Christmas feast and his coming in judgement at the end of time. The scriptural texts should be expounded with this double sense in mind. In a given text one or the other of these comings may be to the fore, but in fact often the same passage provides us with words and images to ponder on both comings at once. And there is another coming as well:

we listen to these readings in the eucharistic assembly, where Christ is truly present. At the beginning of the Advent season, the Church calls to mind St Bernard's teaching that between Christ's two visible comings, in history and at the end of time, there is an invisible coming here and now (cf. Office of Readings, Wednesday, Advent week 1), and she makes her own these words of St Charles Borromeo:

> This holy season teaches us that Christ's coming was not only for the benefit of his contemporaries; his power has still to be communicated to us all. We shall share his power, if, through holy faith and the sacraments, we willingly accept the grace Christ earned for us, and live by that grace and in obedience to Christ (Office of Readings, Monday, Advent week 1).

A. *The First Sunday of Advent*

80. The Gospel of the first Sunday of Advent in all three years is one of the synoptic accounts announcing the sudden coming of the Son of Man in glory on a day and at an hour unknown to us. We are urged to be vigilant and alert, to expect fearful signs in the heavens and on earth, not to be caught unawares. It is always striking to begin Advent in this way, for inevitably Advent puts Christmas in mind, and in many places the wider culture is already conjuring up the gentle images of Christ's birth in Bethlehem. But the liturgy takes us to such images by means of others that remind us that the same Lord born in Bethlehem "will come again in glory to judge the living and the dead," as the Creed puts it. On this Sunday it is the preacher's responsibility to remind the Christian people that they need always prepare themselves for this coming and judgement. Indeed, Advent itself is that preparation: his coming at Christmas is intimately connected with his coming on the last day.

81. In all three years the reading from the prophet can be understood as pointing both toward the Lord's final coming in glory and his first coming in "the lowliness of human flesh," which is recalled at Christmas itself. Both Isaiah (Year A) and Jeremiah (Year C) announce that "the days are coming". In the context of this liturgy, the words that follow point to the final times; but they point as well to the coming solemnity of Christmas.

82. What is it that will happen in days to come? Isaiah says (Year A): "In days to come, the mountain of the Lord's house shall be established as the highest mountain... All nations shall stream toward it..." The homilist has several possible interpretations that could be developed on such a verse. "The mountain of the Lord's house" might well be explained as an image of the Church, to which all nations are destined to be joined. But it can likewise serve as a first announcement of the coming feast of Christmas. "All nations shall stream" toward the child in the manger, a text that will be fulfilled especially on Epiphany when Magi come to worship him. A homilist could remind his own people that they too are among the many nations that are streaming toward Christ, a movement that begins with renewed intensity on this first Sunday of Advent. Even so, the same inspired words apply also to the coming at the end of time that the Gospel names explicitly. The prophet continues, "He [the Lord] shall judge between nations, and impose terms on many peoples." The final words of this prophetic passage are at one at the same time a beautiful summons to the Christmas celebration and a summons to await the coming of the Son of Man in glory: "O house of Jacob, come, let us walk in the light of the Lord."

83. The first reading from Isaiah in Year B is in the form of a prayer that instructs the Church in penitential attitudes that are proper to this season. It begins by expressing a problem, the problem of our sin. "Why do you let us wander, O Lord, from your ways, and harden our hearts so that we fear you not?" This most certainly is a question that needs to be faced. The mystery of human iniquity (cf. *2 Thess* 2:7) – who can understand it? Our experience of it in ourselves and in the world around us – let the homilist give examples – can only summon from our depths a huge cry addressed to God: "Oh, that you would rend the heavens and come down, with the mountains quaking before you!" In Jesus Christ this cry is definitively answered. In him God did rend the heavens and come down. And in him, as the prophet had asked, God "wrought awesome deeds we could not hope for, such as they had not heard of from of old." Christmas is the celebration of the awesome deeds of God we could not have hoped for.

84. Yet on this first Sunday of Advent the Church also has her eye on Jesus's coming again in glory and majesty. "Oh, that you would rend the

heavens and come down, with the mountains quaking before you!" In these same tones the Evangelists describe that final coming. And are we ready for it? No, we are very much in need of a season of preparation. The prophet's prayer continues: "O Lord, would that you might meet us doing right, that we were mindful of you in your ways." Something similar is asked for in the Collect for this Sunday: "Grant your faithful, O God, the resolve to run forth to meet your Christ with righteous deeds at his coming..."

85. In St Luke's gospel, used in Year C, the images are especially vivid. Jesus foretells that in the very midst of many fearful signs that will appear, there shall be a sign that eclipses them all; namely, the appearance of himself as the Lord of Glory. He says, "And then they will see the Son of Man coming in a cloud with power and great glory." For us who belong to him that is not meant to be a day in which we cower in fear. On the contrary, he tells us, "But when these signs begin to happen, stand erect and raise your heads because your redemption is at hand." A homilist well might ask aloud, what would be necessary for us to adopt such an attitude of confidence on the final day? Certainly, it would require some preparation, it would require some change in our lives. It requires in fact this Advent season when we must put into practice the Lord's advice, "Beware that your hearts do not become drowsy. Be vigilant at all times and pray that you have the strength to escape the tribulations that are imminent and to stand before the Son of Man."

86. The Eucharist itself which is about to be celebrated is, of course, the most intense preparation the community has for the Lord's coming, for it is itself his coming. In the preface that begins the Eucharistic Prayer on this Sunday, the community presents itself before God as "we who watch." We who watch ask that already today we may sing the hymn of all the angels: "Holy, Holy, Holy Lord God of hosts." In proclaiming the Mystery of Faith we express the same spirit of watching: "When we eat this bread and drink this cup, we proclaim your death, O Lord, until you come again." In the Eucharistic Prayer the heavens are rent open and God comes down. In Holy Communion the heavens are rent open and God comes down. The one whose Body and Blood we receive today is the Son of Man who will come in a cloud with power and great glory. With

his grace delivered in Holy Communion it may be hoped that each one of us can exclaim, "I will 'stand erect and raise my head, because my redemption is at hand'."

B. The Second and Third Sundays of Advent

87. The figure of St John the Baptist dominates the Gospels of all three cycles on the Second and Third Sundays of Advent. Not only that, he is also often the subject of the Gospel passages of the weekday lectionary in the weeks that follow these Sundays. Further, on December 19, 21, 23, and 24 the Gospel passages all focus on events surrounding John's birth. Finally, the feast of Jesus's baptism by John closes the whole Christmas cycle. What is said here is meant to help the homilist on all these occasions when John the Baptist appears so prominently in the biblical text.

88. That master theologian of the third century, Origen, observed a pattern that contains a great mystery: whenever the Lord Jesus came, he was preceded in that coming by John the Baptist (*Homilies on Luke* IV, 6). Thus it was that even in the womb John leapt to announce the presence of the Lord. In the deserts of the Jordan, John's preaching heralded the one who was to come after him. When he baptised Jesus in the Jordan, the heavens were opened, the Holy Spirit came down upon Jesus in visible form and a voice from heaven declared him to be the Father's beloved Son. John's death was the signal to Jesus to set his face on going up to Jerusalem, where he knew his own death awaited him. John is the last and greatest of the prophets; for after he speaks, the one whom all the prophets foretold comes and acts for our salvation.

89. The same divine Word that once came in the flesh in Palestine comes also to each generation of believing Christians. And John, who preceded Jesus's coming in history, still precedes his coming to us. In the communion of the saints John is present in our assemblies in these days, announcing one who is to come and consequently urging us to repent. This is why every morning the Church sings at Morning Prayer the song that John's father, Zachary, sang at his birth: "You, little child, will go before the Lord to prepare his way, to give his people knowledge of salvation by the forgiveness of their sins" (*Lk* 1:76-77).

90. The homilist should make certain that the Christian people, as part of their preparation for the Lord's twofold coming, hear John's insistent urgings to repentance that are brought to the fore especially in the Gospels on the Second and Third Sundays of Advent. But we hear John's voice not only in the passages of the Gospel; the voices of all the prophets of Israel are gathered together now into the one voice of John. "He is Elijah!" Jesus himself said of him (*Mt* 11:14). Or it could be said, apropos of any of the first readings in the cycles of these Sundays, he is Isaiah, Baruch, Zephaniah. Any prophet's oracle proclaimed in the liturgical assembly of these days is for the Church an echo of John's voice, which prepares here and now the way of the Lord. We are prepared for the coming of the Son of Man in glory and majesty on the last day. We are prepared for this year's Christmas feast.

91. For example, every assembly where the Scriptures are proclaimed is the "Jerusalem" of the prophet Baruch's text (Second Sunday, C): "Jerusalem, take off your robe of mourning and misery; put on the splendour of glory from God forever." Here is a prophet who invites us to a very precise preparation and calls for conversion: "Wrapped in justice, bear on your head the mitre that displays the glory of the eternal name." In the Church the Word made flesh will dwell, and so she is addressed in the words: "Up, Jerusalem! Stand upon the heights; look to the east and see your children gathered from the east and the west at the word of the Holy One, rejoicing that they are remembered by God."

92. Various classic Messianic prophecies of Isaiah are read on these Sundays. "On that day, a shoot shall sprout from the stump of Jesse, and from his roots a bud shall blossom" (*Is* 11:1, Second Sunday, A). The text is fulfilled in the birth of Jesus. Or in a different year, "A voice cries out: In the desert prepare the way of the Lord" (*Is* 40:3, Second Sunday, B). All four of the evangelists see this text fulfilled in John's desert preaching. The same Isaiah text continues "Then the glory of the Lord shall be revealed, and all people shall see it together" (*Is* 40:5). This is said of the final day. This is said of the Christmas feast.

93. On the many occasions when John the Baptist figures in the Gospel, it is striking how often the core of his message about Jesus is repeated: "I have baptised you with water; he will baptise you with the Holy Spirit"

(*Mk* 1:8, Second Sunday B). The baptism with the Holy Spirit that Jesus brings is the direct link between all the texts discussed here and the centre to which this *Directory* has continually pointed; that is, the Paschal Mystery, ultimately fulfilled in Pentecost with the outpouring of the Holy Spirit on all who believe in Christ. The Paschal Mystery is prepared for by the coming of the Only Begotten Son in the flesh, and its infinite riches will be even further displayed on the last day. Isaiah says of the child born in the stable and of the one who will come on the clouds, "The spirit of the Lord shall rest upon him" (*Is* 11:2, Second Sunday A). Or again, using words that Jesus himself will declare to be fulfilled in him, "The spirit of the Lord God is upon me, because the Lord has anointed me; he has sent me to bring glad tidings to the poor" (*Is* 61:1, Third Sunday B. Cf. *Lk* 4:16-21).

94. The Advent Lectionary is in fact a thrilling collection of Old Testament texts that mysteriously find their fulfilment in the coming of the Son of God in the flesh. Again and again the homilist can use the poetry of the prophets to describe for the Christian people the very mysteries into which the liturgies insert them. Christ is continually coming, and the dimensions of this coming are manifold. He has come. He will come again in glory. He comes at Christmas. He comes already now in each Eucharist celebrated during Advent. To all these dimensions the force of the prophets' poetry can be applied: "Here is your God, he comes with vindication; with divine recompense he comes to save you" (*Is* 35:4, Third Sunday A). "Fear not, O Zion, be not discouraged! The Lord, your God, is in your midst, a mighty saviour" (*Zeph* 3:16-17, Third Sunday C). "Comfort, give comfort to my people, says your God. Speak tenderly to Jerusalem, and proclaim to her that her service is at an end, her guilt is expiated" (*Is* 40:1-2, Second Sunday B).

95. It is not surprising, then, as the spirit of anticipation grows through the weeks of Advent, that on the third Sunday the celebrants are clothed in the quietly joyful rose-coloured vestments, and this Sunday takes its name from the first words of the Entrance Song which have for centuries been sung on this day, St Paul's words to the Philippians: "*Gaudete* – Rejoice in the Lord always; again I say, rejoice. Indeed, the Lord is near." He has come. He will come again in glory. He comes at Christmas. He comes already now in each Eucharist celebrated during Advent. "Indeed, the Lord is near."

C. The Fourth Sunday of Advent

96. By the Fourth Sunday of Advent Christmas is very near. The mood of the liturgy shifts from the intense calls to conversion to a focus on the events immediately surrounding the birth of Jesus, a shift highlighted in the second preface for the Advent season. "Behold, the virgin shall conceive," reads the title of the first reading in Year A. And indeed, all the readings– from the prophets, from the Apostles, from the Gospels– cluster around the mystery announced to Mary by the angel Gabriel. (What is said here of the Sunday Gospels and the Old Testament texts can also be applied to the weekday Lectionary of December 17 to 23.)

97. Luke's account of the Annunciation is the Gospel reading in Year B; it is followed in his Gospel by the Visitation, the Gospel reading for Year C. These events have a special place in the devotional life of many Catholics. The first half of one of our most treasured prayers, the Hail Mary, consists of words addressed to Mary by the angel Gabriel and Elizabeth. The Annunciation is the first joyful mystery of the rosary; the Visitation, the second. The prayer of the Angelus is an expanded meditation on the Annunciation, prayed by many of the faithful each day – morning, noon, and night. Some of the greatest art in the history of the Christian faith portrays the encounter between Mary and the Angel with the Holy Spirit coming down upon her. On the Fourth Sunday of Advent the homilist should build upon this firm foundation of Christian devotion and lead his people into a deeper penetration of these wondrous episodes.

98. "The Angel of the Lord declared unto Mary. And she conceived of the Holy Spirit." The power and force of that hour never fade. It is felt anew, pervading the actual assembly where the Gospel is proclaimed. It shapes the precise hour of worship together. We become absorbed in its mystery. We ourselves are somehow present within the scene. We see an angel standing before the Virgin Mary in Nazareth of Galilee – and the Church is assisting at the scene, following with wonder the drama of their encounter, their exchange of words. Divine message, human response. But as we watch, we become aware that we are not allowed this vision as mere passive observers. What is offered to Mary – that she should bear the Son of God in her very body – is also somehow offered in the

liturgy of the Fourth Sunday of Advent to every assembly of the Christian faithful and to every individual believer. Christmas, a few days away, is being offered. It is as Jesus once said: "Anyone who loves me will be true to my word, and my Father will love him; we will come to him and make our dwelling place with him" (*Jn* 14:23).

99. The first reading in Year B, from the Second Book of Samuel, invites us to step back from this scene even while keeping our gaze fixed on it. The reading provides the bigger picture, the history of the dynasty of David. And we are meant to peer through the centuries of this history, seeing at the end of them the angel standing before Mary. It is useful, then, for the homilist to help people to view the whole set of the drama. Generous David is inspired by a noble thought, that of building a house for the Lord. Why, David reasons, now that he is settled and given rest from his enemies on every side, why should the Lord continue to live in the portable shrine of the ark? Why not a house, a temple for the presence of the Lord? But the Lord gives David a most unexpected answer. To David's generous offer he responds with his own divine generosity and thus exceeds utterly what David offered or could even imagine. Turning David's offer on its head, the Lord says in effect, "You will not build a house for me; I will build the house for you" (cf. *2 Sam* 7:11). And by this he meant a dynasty for David that would "endure until the sun fades away and the moon is no more" (*Ps* 72:5).

100. Now, returning to the central scene of this drama, we see that this promise made to David is fulfilled in a definitive way and once again from an unexpected angle. Mary is "betrothed to a man named Joseph, of the house of David" (*Lk* 1:27). Of the child whom the angel asks Mary to bear, it is said, "The Lord God will give him the throne of David his father" (*Lk* 1:32). So Mary herself is the house the Lord builds for David, for David's definitive Son. Yet David's desire of building a house for the Lord is also mysteriously fulfilled: with her "Let it be done unto me according to your word" (*Lk* 1:38) the Daughter of Sion constructs in an instant by her acquiescence in faith a temple worthy of the Son of the Most High God.

58

101. The same mystery of Mary's virginal conception is the subject of the Gospel also in Year A, but the story is told from Joseph's perspective, as recounted in Matthew's Gospel. The first reading on that day is a brief passage from Isaiah where the prophet utters the well known line "the virgin shall conceive, and bear a son, and shall name him Emmanuel." This reading could provide the occasion for the homilist to explain how the Church justifiably sees the fulfilment of Old Testament texts in the events of the life of Jesus. In the passage from Matthew, the assembly hears details surrounding Jesus's birth carefully reported, ending with this phrase: "All this took place to fulfil what the Lord has said through his prophet." A prophet speaks in history, in concrete circumstances. In the year 734 BC King Ahaz was facing a very powerful enemy; the prophet Isaiah urged Ahaz to have faith in the Lord's power to deliver Jerusalem, and he offered the king a sign from the Lord. When the king hypocritically refused, Isaiah angrily proclaimed that a sign would be given him anyway, the sign of a virgin with child whose name shall be called Emmanuel. But now through the Holy Spirit, who spoke through that prophet, what had its sense in those precise historical circumstances expands to accommodate a far greater historical circumstance; namely, the coming of the Son of God in very flesh. All prophecy and all history ultimately speak to that.

102. With this in mind, the homilist can look at Matthew's carefully constructed account. He is concerned to keep in balance two truths about Jesus: that he is Son of David and that he is Son of God. Each is essential for understanding who Jesus is. And both Mary and Joseph play a role in accomplishing this harmonious grasp of the mystery.

103. As we looked at the Annunciation within the context of Israel's history, so here the genealogy that precedes this Gospel gives an important key to its meaning. (The genealogy is read on December 17 and at the Vigil Mass for Christmas.) Matthew's Gospel begins solemnly with these words: "The book of the genealogy of Jesus Christ, the son of David, the son of Abraham." Then the many generations are recounted in the traditional way: Abraham begot Isaac, Isaac begot Jacob, and so forth, through David and his descendants, all the way to Joseph, where the language abruptly and noticeably changes. "Jacob begot Joseph, the

husband of Mary, of whom Jesus was born, who is called Christ." It is striking that the text does not just go on to say, "Joseph begot Jesus," but only that Joseph was the husband of Mary, of whom Jesus was born. It is exactly here that the passage read on the Fourth Sunday begins, and this indicates how its first line is to be understood: "This is how the birth of Jesus Christ came about." That is, in circumstances considerably different from all the previous births, and so requiring now this special account.

104. The first thing we are told is that Mary, *before* she and Joseph came together, is found to be with child by the Holy Spirit. So it is clear to hearers and readers of the passage that the child is not Joseph's, but rather God's own Son. However, in the story this is not yet clear to Joseph. The homilist could note the drama that faced him. Did he suspect Mary of infidelity, and so decide "to divorce her quietly"? Or did he somehow suspect a divine hand at work, making him afraid to take Mary as his wife? What is also puzzling is the silence of Mary. She in fact keeps the secret that is held between her and God, and it will be for God to act to clarify the situation. A human word would not suffice to explain so great a mystery. As Joseph considered these things, an angel reveals to him in a dream that Mary has conceived by the power of the Holy Spirit and that he should not be afraid. The Advent liturgy invites the faithful to fear not, and, like Joseph, to accept the divine mystery that is unfolding in their lives.

105. An angel in a dream confirms for Joseph that Mary has conceived by the Holy Spirit. And so again the point is made: Jesus is Son of God. But Joseph is to do two things, two things that will legitimate the birth of Jesus in the eyes of Jewish culture and faith. He is addressed – pointedly – by the angel as "Joseph, Son of David," and is told to take Mary into his home, allowing her mystery to transform him. Then he is to name the child. Both of these actions make Jesus "Son of David." Matthew's story could have continued with the line "When Joseph awoke, he did as the angel had directed him," but first he interrupts his account with the Isaiah prophecy. "All this took place," he says, "to fulfil what the Lord has said through the prophet." Then he quotes the line from the prophet heard in the first reading. What Isaiah said to Ahaz is small by comparison. Now the word "virgin" is to be taken literally, and she conceives by the Holy Spirit. And what of this name they shall give the child, Emmanuel?

Matthew, unlike Isaiah, spells out what it means: God with us. And this too, the circumstances show us, is to be taken literally. Joseph, the Son of David, will name him Jesus; but the deepest mystery of his name is "God with us."

106. On this same Sunday, in the second reading from the letter to the Romans, a theological language older and more primitive than Matthew's is heard. But already there the importance is clear of the harmonious balance in the titles that express the mystery of Jesus. St Paul speaks of "the gospel concerning God's Son, who was descended from David according to the flesh but established as Son of God in power... by his resurrection from the dead." St Paul sees the title "Son of God" confirmed in Jesus's resurrection. St Matthew, as we just saw, when he explains the name of Emmanuel as meaning "God is with us", expresses this insight about the risen Lord by referring to the beginning of his human existence!

107. Nonetheless, it is Paul who shows a way of bringing all that is heard in these texts directly to bear on ourselves. Having solemnly named the one who is centre of his Gospel "Son of David and Son of God," Paul then names the Gentiles as those "called to belong to Jesus Christ." More, he calls them "beloved of God and called to be holy." The homilist must show that this language is meant to apply also to us. The Christian people hear the wonderful story of the birth of Jesus Christ which marvellously fulfils what was promised through the prophets, but then they hear as well language about themselves: they are called to belong to Jesus Christ; they are beloved of God; they are called to be holy.

108. In Year C the Gospel story relates what Mary did immediately after the encounter with the angel at whose word she conceived. "Mary set out and travelled to the hill country in haste" to find her kinswoman Elizabeth, who was pregnant with John the Baptist. At the sound of Mary's greeting, the infant leapt in Elizabeth's womb. This is the first of John's many announcements of the presence of Jesus. However, it is also instructive to ponder what Mary does when she realises she is carrying the Son of God in her womb. She "hastens" to visit Elizabeth so that she may see that "nothing is impossible with God"; and in so doing she brings Elizabeth and the child in her womb enormous joy.

109. In these final days of Advent the whole Church takes on Marian features. The countenance of the Church is stamped with all the marks of the Virgin. The Holy Spirit is at work in the Church now as he has always worked. Thus, as the assembly enters into the eucharistic mystery on this Sunday, the priest prays in the Prayer over the Offerings, "May the Holy Spirit, O Lord, sanctify these gifts laid upon your altar, just as he filled with his power the womb of the Blessed Virgin Mary." The homilist must draw the same connection that this prayer draws: through the Eucharist, by the power of the Holy Spirit, the faithful will carry in their own bodies what Mary carried in her womb. Like her, they must "hasten" to do good to others. Then their good deeds, like hers, will surprise others with the presence of Christ and cause something within them to leap for joy.

IV. THE CHRISTMAS SEASON

A. *The Liturgies of Christmas*

110. "For the Vigil and the three Masses of Christmas both the prophetic readings and the others have been chosen from the Roman tradition" (OLM 95). A distinctive feature of the solemnity of the Lord's Nativity is the custom of celebrating three different Masses: at midnight, at dawn, and during the day. In the reforms since the Second Vatican Council, an earlier vigil Mass has been added. Apart from monastic communities, it is unlikely that everyone would participate in all three (or four) celebrations; most people will attend one liturgy, which will be their "Christmas Mass". This is why provision is made to choose from among the various readings for any given celebration. Nonetheless, it is instructive to examine the sequence of the four Masses before considering some overarching themes common to all the liturgical and biblical texts.

111. Christmas is a feast of light. It is commonly said that the celebration of the Lord's birth was established in late December to give a Christian meaning to the pagan feast of *Sol invictus*. This may or may not be so, as already in the first part of the third century Tertullian writes that Christ was conceived on March 25th, which, in some calendars, marked the first day of the year. Thus it may be that the Christmas feast was calculated from that date. In any case, beginning in the fourth century many Fathers

recognised the symbolic value of the fact that for them the days grew longer after the feast of the Nativity. Pagan feasts of light in the dark of winter were not uncommon, and winter festivals of light are still sometimes celebrated by nonbelievers today. In contrast to all these, the readings and prayers for the various Christmas liturgies underscore the theme of the true Light who comes to us in Jesus Christ. The first preface for Christmas exclaims, addressing God the Father: "For in the mystery of the Word made flesh a new light of your glory has shone upon the eyes of our mind". The homilist should be attentive to this dynamic of light in darkness that pervades these joyful days. In what follows here the characteristics of each liturgy will be presented briefly.

112. The Vigil Mass: although the celebration of Christmas begins with this liturgy, its prayers and readings evoke a sense of eager anticipation; in a sense, this Mass is a distillation of the entire Advent season. Virtually all of the prayers are in the future tense: "In the morning you will see his glory" (Entrance Antiphon); "We wait in hope for your redemption" (Collect); "Tomorrow the wickedness of the world will be destroyed" (Alleluia verse); "As we look forward, O Lord, to the coming festivities" (Prayer over the Offerings); "The glory of the Lord will be revealed" (Communion antiphon). The readings from Isaiah in the other Christmas Masses describe what *is* happening, while the passage proclaimed at this Mass tells of what *will* happen. The second reading and the Gospel speak of Jesus as the Son of David, and of the human antecedents who prepared the way for his coming. The genealogy from St Matthew's Gospel is akin to the Old Testament lessons at the Easter Vigil, sketching the long path of salvation history that leads to the event we are about to celebrate. The litany of names increases the feeling of suspense; at the Vigil Mass, we are like children clutching a Christmas present, awaiting the word that will allow us to open it.

113. The Mass at Midnight: and, in the middle of the night, while the rest of the world sleeps, Christians open that present, the gift of the Word made flesh. The prophet Isaiah proclaims: "The people who walked in darkness have seen a great light!" He goes on to speak of the glorious victory of the conquering hero who smashes the slave-driver's rod and consigns to the flames all the implements of war. He announces that this ruler's dominion is vast and for ever peaceful, and then heaps upon him title after title: "Wonder-

Counsellor, God-Hero, Father-Forever, Prince of Peace." The beginning
of the Gospel underscores the eminence of this dignitary by naming the
emperor and governor who are reigning when he appears on the scene.
There follows the stunning announcement that this mighty ruler was born
in a modest village on the fringe of the Roman Empire, and that his mother
"wrapped him in swaddling clothes and laid him in a manger, because
there was no room for them in the inn." All of the paradoxes of the Gospel
are suggested by the contrast between the conquering hero described by
Isaiah and the powerless Infant in the crib. The awareness of this paradox
is planted deep in the hearts of our people, and draws them to church at this
late hour. And the fitting response is to join our thanksgiving to that of the
angels, whose song resounds through the heavens on this night.

114. The Mass at Dawn: the readings provided for this liturgy are notably
terse. We are like people awakening to the cold light of day, wondering
if the angelic apparition in the middle of the night was but a dream. The
shepherds, with that direct common sense of the poor, say to one another:
"Let us go, then, to Bethlehem to see this thing that has taken place, which
the Lord has made known to us." They go in haste, and find it just as the
angel had said: there is a poor couple, and their newborn Child asleep
in a trough for feeding animals. Their reaction to this scene of humble
poverty? They return, glorifying and praising God for what they have
heard and seen, and all who hear of it are amazed by what has been told
them. The shepherds see, and we are invited to see, something far more
important than the sentimental scene that has been the subject of so many
artistic representations; but this reality can be perceived only with the
eyes of faith, and it emerges into the light of day at the next liturgy.

115. Mass during the Day: like a brilliant sun fully risen into the sky, the
Prologue of John's Gospel sheds light on the identity of the Infant in the
manger. The Evangelist declares: "The Word became flesh and made his
dwelling among us, and we saw his glory, the glory as of the Father's
only Son, full of grace and truth." In former times, the second reading
reminds us, God spoke in partial and various ways through the prophets;
but now, "In these last days, he has spoken to us through the Son, whom
he made heir of all things and through whom he created the universe, who
is the refulgence of his glory...." Such is his greatness that the very angels

worship him. The invitation is sent out for the whole world to join them: "Come, you nations, and adore the Lord. For today a great light has come upon the earth" (Gospel verse).

116. The reason the Word became flesh was to redeem us by shedding his Blood and to raise us up with him to the glory of the Resurrection. The first disciples recognised the intimate bond between the Incarnation and the Paschal Mystery, as the hymn quoted by St Paul in Philippians 2:5-11 testifies. The light of Midnight Mass is the light of the Easter Vigil. The Collects for these two great solemnities begin in remarkably similar terms: at Christmas, the priest prays, "O God, who have made this most sacred night radiant with the splendour of the true light ..."; and at Easter, "O God, who make this most sacred night radiant with the glory of the Lord's Resurrection...". The second reading of the Mass at Dawn presents an admirable summary of the revelation of the mystery of the Trinity and our insertion into that mystery through baptism: "When the kindness and generous love of God our saviour appeared ... he saved us through the bath of rebirth and renewal by the Holy Spirit, whom he richly poured out on us through Jesus Christ our saviour, so that we might be justified by his grace and become heirs in hope of eternal life." The proper prayers for Mass during the Day speak of Christ as the author of divine generation for us, whose birth manifests the reconciliation that makes us pleasing in God's sight; and the Collect, one of the oldest in the treasury of the Church's prayers, expresses succinctly *why* the Word became flesh: "O God, who wonderfully created the dignity of human nature and still more wonderfully restored it, grant, we pray, that we may share in the divinity of Christ, who humbled himself to share in our humanity." A fundamental purpose of the homily is, as this *Directory* has noted often, to proclaim Christ's Paschal Mystery; the texts of Christmas explicitly provide opportunities to do this.

117. Another purpose of the homily is to lead the community to the Eucharistic sacrifice, wherein the Paschal Mystery becomes present. A powerful signpost here is the word "today" that recurs frequently in the liturgical texts for the Masses of Christmas. The mystery of Christ's birth is present in this celebration, but like his first coming it can be seen only with the eyes of faith. The great "sign" for the shepherds was simply a

poor baby lying in a manger, yet they returned glorifying and praising God for what they had seen. We must perceive with the eyes of faith the same Christ born today under the forms of bread and wine. The "*admirabile commercium*" spoken of in the Collect for Christmas Day, whereby Christ shares in our humanity and we share in his divinity, is manifested in a particular way in the Eucharist, as the prayers for this feast suggest. At Midnight we pray over our Offerings, "May the oblation of today's feast be pleasing to you ... that through this most holy exchange we may be found in the likeness of Christ, in whom our nature is united to you." And at Dawn: "May our offerings be worthy ... of the mysteries of the Nativity this day, that, just as Christ was born a man and also shone forth as God, so these earthly gifts may confer on us what is divine." And again, in Preface III for the Nativity: "For through him the holy exchange that restores our life has shone forth today in splendour: when our frailty is assumed by your Word not only does human mortality receive unending honour but by this wondrous union we, too, are made eternal."

118. That reference to eternity touches on another theme running through the texts of Christmas: our celebration is but a momentary pause on our pilgrimage. The eschatological message so prominent in the season of Advent finds expression here, too. In the Collect for the Vigil we pray "that, as we joyfully welcome your Only Begotten Son as our Redeemer, we may also merit to face him confidently when he comes again as our Judge." In the second reading at Midnight, the Apostle exhorts us "... to live temperately, justly, and devoutly in this age, as we await the blessed hope, the appearance of the glory of our great God and saviour Jesus Christ...." Finally, in the Prayer after Communion for the Mass during the Day we ask God that Christ, born this day, who is the author of divine generation in us "may be the giver even of immortality".

119. The readings and prayers of Christmas provide rich fare for God's people on their pilgrimage through life; they reveal Christ as the Light of the world and invite us to enter into the Paschal Mystery of our redemption through the "today" of our Eucharistic celebration. The homilist can present this banquet to God's people who gather to celebrate the Lord's birth, urging them to imitate Mary, the Mother of Jesus, who "kept all these things, reflecting on them in her heart" (Gospel, Mass at Dawn).

B. *The Feast of the Holy Family*

120. "The Gospel on the Sunday within the Octave of Christmas, Feast of the Holy Family, is about Jesus's childhood and the other readings are about the virtues of family life" (OLM 95). The Evangelists relate practically nothing about the life of Jesus from his birth until the beginning of his public ministry; what little they have passed on to us makes up the selection of Gospel passages for this feast. The portents surrounding the birth of the Saviour fade away, and the Holy Family lives a very ordinary domestic life. As such, they can provide a model for families to imitate, as the prayers for this celebration suggest.

121. The institution of the family faces great challenges in various parts of the world today, and it is entirely appropriate for the homilist to speak about these. However, rather than simply giving a moral exhortation on family values, the preacher should take his cue from the Scripture readings of this day to speak of the Christian family as a school of *discipleship.* Christ, whose birth we are celebrating, came into the world to do the will of his Father, such an obedience that is docile towards the movements of the Holy Spirit has a place in the life of every Christian family. Joseph obeys the angel and takes the Child and his Mother into Egypt (Year A); Mary and Joseph obey the Law by presenting their Baby in the Temple (Year B) and going on pilgrimage to Jerusalem for the feast of Passover (Year C); Jesus for his part is obedient to his earthly parents, but his desire to be in his Father's house is even greater (Year C). As Christians, we are also members of another family, which gathers around the family table of the altar to be fed on the sacrifice that came about because Christ was obedient unto death. We should see our own families as a domestic Church in which we put into practice the pattern of self-sacrificing love we encounter in the Eucharist. Thus all Christian families open outward to become part of Jesus's new and larger family: "For whoever does the will of God is my brother and sister and mother" (*Mk* 3:35).

122. This understanding of the Christian meaning of family life assists the preacher in speaking about the reading from St Paul's Letter to the Colossians. The Apostle's instruction that wives should be subordinate to their husbands can be disturbing to people of our day; if the homilist does

not plan to speak about this directive, it might be more prudent to use the shorter version of the reading. However, the difficult passages of Scripture often have the most to teach us, and this reading provides an opportunity for the homilist to address a theme that may be uncongenial to modern ears, but which in fact does make a valuable and necessary point when properly understood. We can gain insight into the meaning of this text by consulting a similar one, *Eph* 5:21-6:4. There also Paul is speaking about the mutual responsibilities of family life. The key sentence is this: "Be subject to one another out of reverence for Christ" (*Eph* 5:21). The originality of the Apostle's teaching is not that wives should be submissive to their husbands; that was simply presumed in the culture of his day. What is new, and distinctively Christian, is, first, that such submission should be mutual: if the wife is to obey her husband, the husband in turn should, like Christ, lay down his very life for his wife. Secondly, the motive for this mutual subordination is not simply for the sake of harmony in the family or the good of society: no, it is made *out of reverence for Christ*. In other words, mutual submission in the family is an expression of Christian discipleship; the family home is, or should be, a place where we manifest our love for God by laying down our lives for one another. The homilist can challenge his hearers to make real in their own relationships that self-sacrificial love which is at the heart of Christ's life and mission, and which we celebrate in our "family meal" of the Eucharist.

C. The Solemnity of Mary, the Mother of God

123. "On the Octave Day of Christmas, Solemnity of the Blessed Virgin Mary, the Mother of God, the readings are about the Virgin Mother of God and the giving of the holy Name of Jesus" (OLM 95). The week-long celebration of the Christmas feast concludes with this solemnity, which also marks the beginning of the New Year in many parts of the world. The readings and prayers offer an opportunity to consider again the identity of the Child whose birth we are celebrating. He is true God and true Man; the ancient title of *Theotokos* (Mother of God) affirms both the human and divine natures of Christ. He is also our Saviour (*Jesus*, the name he receives at his circumcision, but which was given him by the angel before his conception). He saves us being born under the Law and ransoming us

by the shedding of his Blood: the rite of circumcision celebrates Jesus's entrance into the covenant and foreshadows "the Blood of the new and eternal covenant, which will be poured out for you and for many for the forgiveness of sins". Mary's role in the work of salvation is also a central theme in this liturgy, both in relation to Christ, who received his human nature from her, and in relation to the members of his Body: she is the Mother of the Church who intercedes for us. Finally, the celebration of the New Year provides an occasion to give thanks for the blessings of the year just ended, and to pray that in the year ahead we, like Mary, will cooperate with God in the ongoing mission of Christ. The Prayer over the Offerings brings these various strands together very well: "O God, who in your kindness begin all good things and bring them to fulfilment, grant to us, who find joy in the Solemnity of the holy Mother of God, that, just as we glory in the beginnings of your grace, so one day we may rejoice in its completion. Through Christ our Lord."

D. The Solemnity of the Epiphany

124. The threefold dimension of Epiphany (the visit of the Magi, Christ's Baptism and the miracle at Cana) is especially evident in the Liturgy of the Hours on Epiphany and in the days surrounding the solemnity. But in the Latin tradition the Eucharistic liturgy focuses on the Gospel story of the Magi. A week later, the feast of the Baptism of the Lord focuses on that dimension of the Lord's Epiphany. In Year C the Sunday following the Baptism has as its Gospel the wedding feast at Cana.

125. The three scripture readings of the Epiphany Mass represent three very different genres of biblical literature. The first reading from Isaiah is jubilant poetry. The second reading from St Paul is a precise theological statement delivered in what is virtually technical language for Paul. The Gospel passage is a dramatic narration of events, every detail of which is filled with symbolic meaning. Together they reveal the feast; they define Epiphany. To hear them proclaimed and, with the Spirit's help, to understand them more deeply – this is the Epiphany celebration. God's holy Word unveils before the whole world the ultimate meaning of the birth of Jesus Christ. Christmas, begun on December 25, reaches its climax today in Epiphany: Christ revealed to all the nations.

126. A homilist could begin with the passage from St Paul, a passage that is quite short but extremely intense; it is a precise statement of what Epiphany is. Paul refers to his unique encounter with the risen Jesus on the road to Damascus and all that flows from that. He calls what happened to him there "revelation," that is, not some idea he puts forth as a personal opinion, but rather a completely new and unexpected understanding of things, an understanding delivered with divine authority in an encounter with the Lord Jesus. He also calls this revelation a "grace," and a "stewardship," that is, a treasure that has been entrusted to him for the benefit of others. Further, he calls what was made known to him "the mystery." This "mystery" is something not known in the past, something hidden from our understanding, some meaning hidden in events, but now – and this is Paul's announcement! – now revealed, now made known. And what is that meaning hidden to other generations and now made known? It is this, and this is the Epiphany statement: "the Gentiles are now co-heirs [with the Jews], members of the same body, and co-partners in the promise in Christ Jesus through the Gospel." This is an enormous turnabout in understanding for the zealous Pharisee Saul, who once believed that scrupulous observance of the Jewish law was the only path of salvation. But no, now Paul announces "the Gospel," unexpected good news in Christ Jesus. Yes, Jesus is the fulfilment of all the promises God made to the Jewish people; indeed, he cannot be understood apart from those promises. But now "the Gentiles are co-heirs [with the Jews], members of the same body, and co-partners in the promise in Christ Jesus through the Gospel."

127. In fact, the events reported in Matthew's gospel on Epiphany are the enactment of what Paul is saying here. Magi from the east arrive in Jerusalem summoned by a star. Magi – that is, Gentile religious sages, students of the worthy wisdom traditions in which the human race sought longingly for the unknown Creator and Ruler of all things. They represent all the nations, and they have found their way to Jerusalem, not by following the Jewish scriptures but by following a wonder in the heavens which indicated that something of cosmic significance had taken place. Their non-Jewish wisdom has figured out a fair amount. "We saw his star at its rising and have come to do him homage." Even so, for the final phase of their journey, to arrive at the precise end of all their

searching, they do need the Jewish scriptures, the prophet's identification of Bethlehem as the place of the Messiah's birth. Once this is learned from the Jewish scriptures, the cosmic sign once again indicates the way. "And behold, the star that they had seen at its rising preceded them, until it came and stopped over the place where the child was." In the Magi the entire human race's longing for God arrives in Bethlehem and finds there "the child Jesus with Mary his mother."

128. It is at this point in Matthew's narrative that Isaiah's poem can enter as a comment. Its jubilant tones help us to measure the wonder of this moment. "Rise up in splendour, Jerusalem!" the prophet urges. "Your light has come, the glory of the Lord shines upon you." This text was originally produced in historical circumstances in which the Jewish people needed rousing in a dark chapter of their history. But now, applied to the Magi in the presence of Jesus, it receives a fulfilment beyond what ever could have been imagined. The light, the glory, the splendour – it is the star that leads the Magi. Or, more – it is Jesus himself, "the light of the nations and the glory of his people Israel." "Rise up, Jerusalem," the prophet says. Yes, but now we know through St Paul's revelation that if Jerusalem is addressed – and this is a principle that can be applied anywhere in the Scriptures – it cannot merely mean the historical, earthly city. For, "the Gentiles are now co-heirs [with the Jews]." And so every nation is addressed with the title "Jerusalem." The Church, which is gathered from all the nations, is called "Jerusalem." Every baptised soul in its depths in called "Jerusalem." Thus is fulfilled what was prophesied in the psalm: "Glorious things are said of you, O City of God." And as all the nations are enrolled as citizens of Jerusalem, "They will sing and dance as they say, 'All my origins are in you.'" (*Ps* 87:3, 7).

129. And so on Epiphany every assembly of believing Christians is addressed by the prophet's stirring words. "Your light has come, Jerusalem!" Every worshipper, with the homilist's help, should hear this word in the depths of his or her heart! "See, darkness covers the earth, and thick clouds cover the peoples; but upon you the Lord shines, and over you appears his glory." The homilist here must urge people to leave behind their sluggish ways and visions too short on hope. "Raise your eyes and look about you. They all gather and come to you," that

is, Christians have been given what the whole world is searching for. Caravans of nations will come streaming to the grace in which we already stand. Rightly do we sing in the responsorial psalm, "Lord, every nation on earth will adore you!"

130. Our reflection could return from Isaiah's poem to Matthew's narrative. The Magi model for us how to approach the child. "They prostrated themselves and did him homage." We have entered into this sacred liturgy to do the same. A homilist would do well to remind his people that when they come to communion on Epiphany, they should think of themselves as having at last reached the place and the Person to which the star and the Scriptures have led them. Then let them offer to Jesus the gold of their love for one another. Let them offer to him the frankincense of their faith by which they acknowledge him to be God-with-us. Let them offer to him myrrh, signifying their willingness to die to sin and be buried with him so to rise to life eternal. And then, like the Magi, they could be urged to go home by another route. They can forget Herod, a wicked impostor, and all he ever asked them to do. On this feast they have seen the Lord! "Rise up in splendour. Your light has come. The glory of the Lord shines on you." The homilist might urge them, as St Leo did so many centuries ago, to imitate the service of the star. As the star by its brightness brought the nations to Christ, so this assembly by the brightness of faith, praise, and good deeds should shine in this dark world like a bright star. "Thick clouds cover the peoples, but upon you the Lord shines."

E. The Feast of the Baptism of the Lord

131. The feast of the Baptism of the Lord, a dimension of Epiphany, closes the Christmas season and opens it outward into Ordinary time. When Jesus is baptised by John in the Jordan, something enormous happens. The heavens are torn open then, the Father's voice is heard, and the Spirit is seen coming down in visible form upon Jesus. This is an epiphany of the mystery of the Holy Trinity. But why does such a vision occur in the moment when Jesus is baptised? The homilist must give some answer to this question.

132. The explanation lies in Jesus's purpose in coming to John and being baptised by him. John is preaching a baptism of repentance. Jesus wants to make this sign of repentance together with the many others who were coming to John. At first John tries to prevent him, but Jesus insists. And his insistence expresses what he intends: he means to stand in solidarity with sinners. He means to be where they must be. The same thing is expressed by the Apostle Paul using a different kind of language: "He who knew no sin became sin for our sake" (*2 Cor* 5:21).

133. And it is precisely in this moment of intense solidarity with sinners that this immense trinitarian epiphany takes place. The Father's voice thunders from heaven, declaring, "You are my beloved Son; with you I am well pleased." And we must understand that what pleases the Father is precisely the Son's willingness to stand in solidarity with sinners. In this way he shows himself to be the Son of this Father, this Father "who so loved the world that he gave to it his only Son" (*Jn* 3:16). In the same instant, the Spirit appears like a dove, descending upon the Son, functioning as a sort of accreditation or authorisation of the whole unexpected scene.

134. The Spirit who shaped this scene and indeed prepared for it through the long centuries of Israel's history – "Who spoke through the prophets," as we profess in the Creed – is present to the homilist and his hearers, opening their minds to an ever deeper understanding of the scene. The same Spirit accompanied Jesus in every moment of his earthly existence, shaping each of his actions into a revelation of his Father. Thus, we can hear this morning's text from the prophet Isaiah as an expansion within the heart of Jesus on the Father's words "You are my beloved Son." Their loving dialogue continues: "You are my chosen one with whom I am well pleased, upon whom I have put my Spirit … I the Lord have called you for the victory of justice, I have grasped you by the hand; I formed you and set you as a covenant of the people, a light for the nations."

135. The responsorial psalm on this feast seizes on the words of Psalm 29, "The voice of the Lord is over the waters." The Church sings this psalm as a celebration of the words of the Father which we are privileged to hear and the hearing of which is our feast. "Beloved Son in whom I

am well pleased!" – this is the "voice of the Lord over the waters, over the vast waters. The voice of the Lord is mighty. The voice of the Lord is majestic" (*Ps* 29:3-4).

136. After Jesus's baptism, the Spirit sends him out into the desert to be put to the test by Satan. Then Jesus, still and ever guided by the Spirit, appears in Galilee proclaiming the Kingdom of God. In the course of his spellbinding preaching and his wonderful miracles, Jesus once said, "There is a baptism with which I must be baptised, and how great is my anguish until it is accomplished" (*Lk* 12:50). With these words he referred to his coming death in Jerusalem. In this way we learn that Jesus's baptism by John was not his ultimate baptism but an acting out in symbolic fashion of what he would accomplish in the baptism of his final agony and death on the cross. For it is on the cross that Jesus shows himself, not merely in symbol but in very deed, in complete solidarity with sinners. There he "became sin for us" (*2 Cor* 5:21), there "he was made a curse for us" (*Gal* 3:13). There he went down into the chaos of the waters of the underworld and drowned our sins forever. But from the cross and from his death, Jesus is also brought up from the waters, called to resurrection by the Father's voice which says, "You are my beloved Son. In you I am well pleased. Today I have begotten you" (*Heb* 1:5). This scene of death and resurrection is the masterpiece of the Spirit's writing and direction. The voice of the Lord over the mighty waters of death raises his Son from the dead, majestic and mighty. "The voice of the Lord is mighty. The voice of the Lord is majestic."

137. Jesus's baptism is the pattern also of ours. In baptism we go down with Christ into the waters of death, and our sins are drowned in those waters. And because we have gone down with Christ, we also come up from the waters together with him and hear – mighty and majestic – the Father's voice directed to us as well. It pronounces a new name for each of us, in the depths of each of our hearts: "Beloved! In whom I am well pleased." We hear this name as ours not because of any good deeds we have done but because Christ in his overflowing love willed to share his relationship to his Father with us.

138. The Eucharist that is celebrated on this feast deepens all the patterns of this story. The Spirit appears hovering over the gifts of bread and wine which the faithful bring. The words of Jesus – "This is my body, this is my blood" – announce his intention to receive the baptism of death for our sake. And the assembly prays, "Our Father" together with the Son because it has heard the Father call it "Beloved" together with him.

139. Jesus once said in the course of his ministry, "Whoever believes in me, as scripture says, 'Rivers of living water will flow from within him.'" Those living waters began to flow within each of us at our baptism, and they become an ever stronger river with every celebration of the Eucharist.

V. THE SUNDAYS IN ORDINARY TIME

140. The seasons of Advent, Christmas, Lent, and Easter possess a distinctive character, and the readings chosen for those seasons have an inherent harmony flowing from that character. Such is not the case with the Sundays in Ordinary Time, as the *Introduction of the Lectionary* makes clear: "In contrast, the Sundays in Ordinary Time do not have a distinctive character. Thus the texts of both the apostolic and Gospel readings are arranged in order of semi-continuous reading, whereas the Old Testament reading is harmonised with the Gospel" (OLM 67).

The compilers of the Lectionary intentionally rejected the idea of assigning a "theme" to each Sunday of the year and choosing readings accordingly: "Such an arrangement would be in conflict with the genuine conception of liturgical celebration, which is always the celebration of the mystery of Christ and which by its own tradition makes use of the Word of God not only at the prompting of logical or extrinsic concerns but spurred by the desire to proclaim the Gospel and to lead those who believe to the fulness of truth" (OLM 68).

Faithful to the mandate of the Second Vatican Council, which directed that "the treasures of the Bible are to be opened up more lavishly" (SC 21), the three-year Lectionary for Ordinary Time presents to the faithful the mystery of Christ as recorded in the Gospels of Matthew, Mark, and Luke. The homilist can be aided in his preparation by attending to the structure of the readings in Ordinary Time. The *Directory* here presents what the *Introduction of the Lectionary* says about this structure, beginning with the Gospel.

141. After noting that the Second Sunday of Ordinary Time continues the theme of the Lord's manifestation, celebrated at Epiphany and the Feast of the Baptism of the Lord, the *Introduction* goes on to say:

> Beginning with the Third Sunday, there is a semicontinuous reading of the Synoptic Gospels. This reading is arranged in such a way that as the Lord's life and preaching unfold the doctrine proper to each of these Gospels is presented.
>
> This distribution also provides a certain coordination between the meaning of each Gospel and the progress of the liturgical year. Thus after Epiphany the readings are on the beginning of the Lord's preaching and they fit in well with Christ's baptism and the first events in which he manifests himself. The liturgical year leads quite naturally to a conclusion in the eschatological theme proper to the last Sundays, since the chapters of the Synoptics that precede the account of the Passion treat this eschatological theme rather extensively (105).

Thus there is a common pattern followed in all three cycles: the early weeks deal with the beginning of Christ's public ministry, the final weeks have an eschatological theme, and the intervening weeks take in sequence various events and teachings from our Lord's life.

142. Each year is distinctive as well, because it unfolds the doctrine proper to each of the synoptic Gospels. The homilist should avoid the temptation to approach each Sunday's Gospel passage as an independent entity: awareness of the overall structure and distinctive features of each Gospel can deepen his understanding of the text.

143. YEAR A: the public ministry of Jesus is presented in a very organised way by St Matthew: there are five discourses, each preceded by narrative material. The Lectionary is faithful to this structure. 1. The Sermon on the Mount (4th to 9th Sundays), preceded by the call of the first disciples (3rd Sunday). 2. The Missionary Instruction (11th to 13th Sundays), preceded by the call of Matthew. 3. The Parable Discourse (15th to 17th Sundays), preceded by narrative of the Good News revealed to the simple. 4. The Discourse on the Church (23rd and 24th Sundays), preceded by narratives of miracles, Peter's confession, and the announcement of the Passion. 5. The Eschatological Discourse (32nd to 34th Sundays), preceded by

narratives of parables and incidents involving the acceptance or rejection of the Kingdom. Awareness of this structure enables the homilist to connect what he says about the discourses over a period of several weeks, and also help his people appreciate the integral relationship between Jesus's life and teaching, as the first Evangelist lays this out in his pattern of narratives and discourses.

144. YEAR B: although it does not have the complex organisation of the other two synoptic Gospels, Mark's account possesses its own dynamism, and the homilist can note this from time to time as the year unfolds. The early ministry of Jesus is greeted with great acclaim (3rd to 9th Sundays), but opposition soon arises (10th Sunday). Even his own followers misunderstand him, because their hopes are set on an earthly Messiah; the turning point in Mark's account of the public ministry comes with Peter's confession of faith, Christ's first announcement of his Passion, and Peter's rejection of this plan (24th to 25th Sundays). The misunderstandings that run through this Gospel, as Jesus continues to say and do things that puzzle and scandalise his hearers, provides a salutary lesson to the Christian community as we gather each week to listen to the Word of God – the mystery of Christ always challenges our expectations. Another important feature in Cycle B is the substitution of John's account of the miracle of the loaves and fishes and subsequent Bread of Life discourse (17th to 21st Sundays). This provides an opportunity for the homilist to preach for several weeks on Christ as the living Bread who nourishes us with both his Word and his Body and Blood.

145. YEAR C: The doctrine proper to the Gospel of Luke is above all the gentleness and forgiveness that were the hallmarks of Christ's ministry. From the beginning of his mission until he nears Jerusalem, those who encounter Jesus, from Peter (5th Sunday) to Zacchaeus (31st Sunday) become aware of their need for forgiveness and for God's great mercy. Several stories peculiar to Luke's Gospel illustrate this theme of divine mercy throughout the course of the year: the penitent woman (11th Sunday), the Good Samaritan (15th Sunday), the lost sheep and the prodigal son (24th Sunday), and the good thief (34th Sunday). There are also warnings for those who do not show mercy: maledictions as well as beatitudes (6th Sunday), the rich fool (18th Sunday), and the rich man and

Lazarus (26th Sunday). Written for Gentiles, Luke's Gospel underscores how God's mercy reaches beyond his chosen people to embrace those who were formerly excluded. This theme appears often on these Sundays, and is a warning for us as we gather to celebrate the Eucharist: we have received the bountiful mercy of Christ, and there can be no frontiers to the mercy we share with others.

146. Concerning the Old Testament readings in Ordinary Time, the *Introduction of the Lectionary* says:

> These readings have been chosen to correspond to the Gospel passages in order to avoid an excessive diversity between the readings of different Masses and above all to bring out the unity between the Old and the New Testament. The connection between the readings of the same Mass is shown by a precise choice of the headings prefixed to the individual readings.
>
> To the degree possible, the readings were chosen in such a way that they would be short and easy to grasp. But care has been taken to ensure that many Old Testament texts of major significance would be read on Sundays. Such readings are distributed not according to a logical order but on the basis of what the Gospel reading requires. Still, the treasury of the Word of God will be opened up in such a way that nearly all the principal pages of the Old Testament will become familiar to those taking part in the Mass on Sundays (106).

The examples that have been given in the *Directory* for the seasons of Advent/Christmas and Lent/Easter illustrate ways the homilist can relate the readings from the Old and New Testaments, showing how they converge on the person and mission of Jesus Christ. Nor should the Responsorial Psalm be neglected, because this, too, is chosen to harmonise with the Gospel and Old Testament reading. The homilist must not presume that his people will automatically see these connections; they should be pointed out when preaching. The *Introduction of the Lectionary* also draws attention here to the headings chosen for each reading; elsewhere it explains that they have been chosen carefully to point out the main theme of the reading and, when necessary, to make the connection between the readings of the same Mass clear (cf. 123).

147. Finally, there are the readings from the Apostles in Ordinary Time:

> There is a semicontinuous reading of the Letters of Paul and James (the Letters of Peter and John being read during the Easter and Christmas seasons).
>
> Because it is quite long and deals with such diverse issues, the First Letter to the Corinthians has been spread over the three years of the cycle at the beginning of Ordinary Time. It also was thought best to divide the Letter to the Hebrews into two parts; the first part is read in Year B and the second in Year C.
>
> Only readings that are short and readily grasped by the people have been chosen (OLM 107).

In addition to what is said in the *Introduction of the Lectionary*, two other observations should be made about the arrangement of texts from the Apostles. First, during the final weeks of the Church year we listen to the First and Second Letters to the Thessalonians, which treat of eschatological themes; these harmonise well with the other readings and the liturgical texts of these Sundays. Second, Paul's magisterial Letter to the Romans is a major part of Cycle A, from the 9th to the 25th Sundays. Given the importance of the Letter, and the place devoted to it in the Lectionary, the homilist may want to single it out for special attention during the Sundays of Ordinary Time.

148. It must be recognised that the readings from the Apostles create something of a dilemma, since they are not chosen to harmonise with the Gospel and the Old Testament reading. There are times when they resonate in some explicit way with the other readings. However, they often do not, and the homilist should not do violence to them to make them "agree" with the other selections. It is certainly legitimate for the homilist to preach primarily on the second reading occasionally, and perhaps even devote several Sundays to one of the Letters.

149. The fact that the Sundays in Ordinary Time do not have an inherent harmony can represent a challenge to the preacher, but this challenge provides an opportunity to emphasise yet again the fundamental purpose of the homily: "Through the readings and homily Christ's Paschal Mystery is proclaimed; through the sacrifice of the Mass it becomes present" (OLM 24).

The homilist should not feel the need to say something about each reading, or to build artificial bridges between them: the unifying principle is how Christ's Paschal Mystery is revealed and celebrated at this liturgical gathering. On a given Sunday, the way into that mystery may be suggested by the Gospel reading, seen in light of the doctrine proper to a given Evangelist; this might be enhanced by a reflection on the relationship between the Gospel passage, the Old Testament reading, and the Responsorial Psalm; or he may choose to base his homily primarily on the reading from the Apostle. But in any case, his purpose is not to create a *tour de force* that exhaustively ties together all the various threads in all the readings, but to follow one thread as it leads the people of God into the heart of the mystery of Christ's life, death, and Resurrection which becomes present in the liturgical celebration.

VI. OTHER OCCASIONS

A. Weekday Mass

150. The custom of celebrating the Eucharist daily is a great source of holiness for Catholics of the Roman Rite, and pastors should encourage their people to participate in daily Mass if at all possible. Pope Benedict urges the homilist "to offer at weekday Masses *cum populo* brief and timely reflections which can help the faithful to welcome the Word which was proclaimed and to let it bear fruit in their lives" (VD 59). The daily Eucharist is less solemn than the Sunday liturgy, and it should be celebrated in such a way that people who have responsibilities of family and work can avail themselves of the opportunity to attend daily Mass; hence the need for the homily on such occasions to be brief. On the other hand, because many people come to daily Mass regularly, there is an opportunity for the homilist to preach about a particular book of the Bible over the course of time in a way that the Sunday celebration does not allow.

151. A homily at daily Mass is encouraged particularly in the liturgical seasons of Advent/Christmas and Lent/Easter. The readings for these seasons have been chosen with care, and the principles are given in the *Introduction of the Lectionary*: for Advent, n. 94; for Christmas, n. 96; for Lent, n. 98; for Easter, n. 101. Familiarity with these principles can aid the homilist when preparing his brief daily remarks.

152. The *Introduction of the Lectionary* makes a point about the readings in Ordinary Time to which the preacher must be attentive when preparing weekday liturgies:

> The arrangement of weekday readings provides texts for every day of the week throughout the year. In most cases, therefore, these readings are to be used on their assigned days, unless a solemnity, a feast, or else a memorial with proper readings occurs.
>
> In using the Order of Readings for weekdays attention must be paid to whether one reading or another from the same biblical book will have to be omitted because of some celebration occurring during the week. With the arrangement of readings for the entire week in mind, the priest in that case arranges to omit the less significant passages or combines them in the most appropriate manner with other readings, if they contribute to an integral view of a particular theme (82).

Thus, the homilist is encouraged to review the readings for the entire week and make adaptations to the sequence of readings when it is interrupted by a special celebration. Although the weekday homily is brief, it should be carefully prepared in advance. Experience teaches that a short homily often requires additional preparation.

153. When the Lectionary provides a proper reading for the celebration of a saint, this must be used. In addition, readings may be chosen from the Commons if there is reason to give greater attention to a saint's celebration. But the *Introduction of the Lectionary* cautions:

> The first concern of a priest celebrating with a congregation is the spiritual benefit of the faithful and he will be careful not to impose his personal preference on them. Above all he will make sure not to omit too often or without sufficient cause the readings assigned for each day in the weekday Lectionary: the Church's desire is that a more lavish table of the Word of God be spread before the faithful (83).

B. Weddings

154. Regarding the homily at the celebration of marriage, the *Rite of Marriage* says: "After the reading of the Gospel, the Priest in the homily uses the sacred text to expound the mystery of Christian Marriage, the dignity of conjugal love, the grace of the Sacrament, and the responsibilities of married people, keeping in mind, however, the various circumstances of individuals" (57). Preaching at a wedding presents two unique challenges. The first is that even for many Christians today, marriage is not seen to be a vocation; the "mystery of Christian marriage" must be proclaimed and taught. The second challenge is that very often there are non-Catholics and non-Christians present for the ceremony, so the homilist cannot assume that his hearers are familiar with even the most fundamental elements of Christian faith. These challenges are also opportunities for the preacher to articulate a vision of life and marriage that is rooted in Christian discipleship, and so in the Paschal Mystery of Christ's death and Resurrection. The homilist must prepare carefully so that he can "expound the mystery of Christian Marriage" while "keeping in mind the circumstances of individuals".

C. Funerals

155. The *Order of Christian Funerals* articulates concisely the purpose and the meaning of the homily at a funeral. In the light of the Word of God, while keeping in mind the fact that the homily must avoid the form and style of a eulogy (cf. 141), "priests are to keep in mind with delicate sensitivity not only the identity of the deceased and the circumstances of the death, but also the grief of the bereaved and their needs for a Christian life" (*Introduction of the Order of Christian Funerals* 18 [Latin edition]). The love of God manifested in Christ crucified and risen enlivens faith, hope, and charity, and belief in eternal life and the communion of the saints brings consolation to those who grieve. The circumstances of a funeral offer the opportunity to consider the mystery of life and death, the proper perspective of life on earth as a pilgrimage, the merciful judgment of God, and the never-ending life of heaven.

156. The homilist must show particular concern also for those attending the liturgical celebration on the occasion of a funeral who are non-Catholics or even Catholics who rarely participate at the Eucharist or who appear to have lost the faith (cf. *Introduction of the Order of Christian Funerals* 18 [Latin edition]). The Scripture readings, the prayers, and the chants of the funeral liturgy nourish and express the faith of the Church.

APPENDIX I:

THE HOMILY AND THE *CATECHISM OF THE CATHOLIC CHURCH*

157. A concern that has been voiced often in the years since the Second Vatican Council, notably in Synods of Bishops, has been the need for more doctrine in preaching. The *Catechism of the Catholic Church* provides a truly useful resource for the homilist in this regard, but it is important that it be used in a way that is consonant with the purpose of the homily.

158. The *Roman Catechism* was published at the direction of the Fathers of the Council of Trent, and some editions included a *Praxis Catechismi* which divided the contents of the *Roman Catechism* according to the Gospels for the Sundays of the year. It is not surprising that, with the publication of a new catechism in the wake of the Second Vatican Council, the suggestion has been raised to do something similar with the *Catechism of the Catholic Church*. Such an initiative faces many practical obstacles, but more crucial is the fundamental objection that the Sunday liturgy is not an "occasion" on which to deliver a sermon, that would in its topic be contrary to the liturgical season and its themes. Even so, there may be specific pastoral reasons requiring the explanation of a particular aspect of doctrinal and moral teaching. Decisions of this sort require pastoral prudence.

159. On the other hand, the most important doctrines are located within the deepest sense of Scripture and this deepest sense reveals itself when the Word of God is proclaimed in the liturgical assembly. The homilist's task is not to make the readings at Mass fit a preconceived schema of topics, but to invite his listeners to ponder the faith of the Church as it emerges naturally from the Scriptures in the context of the liturgical celebration.

160. With that in mind, the following table indicates paragraphs in the *Catechism of the Catholic Church* that resonate with the biblical readings for Sundays and holy days. The paragraphs were chosen either because

they cite or allude to the specific readings, or because they treat topics found in the readings. The homilist is encouraged not simply to consult the *Catechism* in a cursory fashion, but to meditate on how its four parts are mutually related. For example, on the Fifth Sunday of Ordinary Time in Year A the first reading speaks of care for the poor, the second about the folly of the Cross, and the third about disciples as the salt of the earth and the light of the world. The citations from the *Catechism* associate these readings with several important themes: Christ crucified is the wisdom of God, contemplated in relation to the problem of evil and God's apparent powerlessness (272); it is in the face of this evil that Christians are called to be the light of the world, and their mission is to be a seed of unity, hope and salvation to the whole human race (782); we become this light by sharing in Christ's Paschal Mystery, symbolised by the Easter candle whose light is given to the newly-baptised (1243); "in order that the message of salvation can show the power of its truth and radiance before men, it must be authenticated by the witness of life of Christians" (2044); and this witness finds a particular expression in our love for the poor (2443-2449). By using the *Catechism of the Catholic Church* in this way, the homilist can help his people integrate the word of God, the faith of the Church, the moral demands of the Gospel, and their personal and liturgical spirituality.

.

CYCLE A

First Sunday of Advent

CCC 668-677, 769: the final tribulation and Christ's return in glory
CCC 451, 671, 1130, 1403, 2817: "Come, Lord Jesus!"
CCC 2729-2733: humble vigilance of heart

Second Sunday of Advent

CCC 522, 711-716, 722: the prophets and the expectation of the Messiah
CCC 523, 717-720: the mission of John the Baptist
CCC 1427-1429: conversion of the baptised

Third Sunday of Advent

CCC 30, 163, 301, 736, 1829, 1832, 2015, 2362: joy
CCC 227, 2613, 2665, 2772: patience
CCC 439, 547-550, 1751: Jesus performs messianic signs

Fourth Sunday of Advent

CCC 496-507, 495: Mary's virginal motherhood
CCC 437, 456, 484-486, 721-726: Mary the Mother of Christ by the Holy Spirit
CCC 1846: Jesus as Saviour revealed to Joseph
CCC 445, 648, 695: Christ the Son of God in his Resurrection
CCC 143-149, 494, 2087: the "obedience of faith"

The Solemnity of Christmas

CCC 456-460, 466: "Why did the Word become flesh?"
CCC 461-463, 470-478: the Incarnation
CCC 437, 525-526: the Christmas mystery
CCC 439, 496, 559, 2616: Jesus is the Son of David
CCC 65, 102: God has said everything in his Word
CCC 333: the incarnate Christ worshipped by the angels
CCC 1159-1162, 2131, 2502: the Incarnation and images of Christ

The Holy Family

CCC 531-534: the Holy Family
CCC 1655-1658, 2204-2206: the Christian family, a domestic Church
CCC 2214-2233: duties of family members
CCC 333, 530: the Flight into Egypt

The Solemnity of Mary, the Mother of God

CCC 464-469: Jesus Christ, true God and true Man
CCC 495, 2677: Mary is the Mother of God
CCC 1, 52, 270, 294, 422, 654, 1709, 2009: our adoption as sons
CCC 527, 577-582: Jesus submits to the Law, and perfects it
CCC 580, 1972: the New Law frees from restrictions of the Old Law
CCC 683, 689, 1695, 2766, 2777-2778: in the Holy Spirit we can call God "Abba"
CCC 430-435, 2666-2668, 2812: the name of Jesus

Second Sunday after the Nativity

CCC 151, 241, 291, 423, 445, 456-463, 504-505, 526, 1216, 2466, 2787: John's Prologue
CCC 272, 295, 299, 474, 721, 1831: Christ the Wisdom of God
CCC 158, 283, 1303, 1831, 2500: God gives us wisdom

The Solemnity of the Epiphany

CCC 528, 724: the Epiphany
CCC 280, 529, 748, 1165, 2466, 2715: Christ the light of the nations
CCC 60, 442, 674, 755, 767, 774-776, 781, 831: the Church, sacrament of human unity

First Sunday of Lent

CCC 394, 538-540, 2119: the temptation of Jesus
CCC 2846-2849: "Lead us not into temptation"
CCC 385-390, 396-400: the Fall
CCC 359, 402-411, 615: Adam, Original Sin, Christ the New Adam

Second Sunday of Lent

CCC 554-556, 568: the Transfiguration
CCC 59, 145-146, 2570-2571: the obedience of Abraham
CCC 706: God's promise to Abraham fulfilled in Christ
CCC 2012-2014, 2028, 2813: the call to holiness

Third Sunday of Lent

CCC 1214-1216, 1226-1228: baptism, rebirth of water and Spirit
CCC 727-729: Jesus reveals the Holy Spirit
CCC 694, 733-736, 1215, 1999, 2652: the Holy Spirit, the living water, a gift of God
CCC 604, 733, 1820, 1825, 1992, 2658: God takes the initiative; hope from the Spirit

Fourth Sunday of Lent

CCC 280, 529, 748, 1165, 2466, 2715: Christ the light of the nations

CCC 439, 496, 559, 2616: Jesus is the Son of David

CCC 1216: baptism is illumination

CCC 782, 1243, 2105: Christians are to be light of the world

Fifth Sunday of Lent

CCC 992-996: the progressive revelation of resurrection

CCC 549, 640, 646: raisings a messianic sign prefiguring Christ's Resurrection

CCC 2603-2604: the prayer of Jesus before the raising of Lazarus

CCC 1002-1004: our present experience of resurrection

CCC 1402-1405, 1524: the Eucharist and the Resurrection

CCC 989-990: the resurrection of the body

Palm Sunday of the Lord's Passion

CCC 557-560: Christ's entry into Jerusalem

CCC 602-618: the Passion of Christ

CCC 2816: Christ's kingship gained through his death and Resurrection

CCC 654, 1067-1068, 1085, 1362: the Paschal Mystery and the liturgy

Thursday of the Lord's Supper

CCC 1337-1344: the institution of the Eucharist

CCC 1359-1361: Eucharist as thanksgiving

CCC 610, 1362-1372, 1382, 1436: Eucharist as sacrifice

CCC 1373-1381: the real presence of Christ in the Eucharist

CCC 1384-1401, 2837: Holy Communion

CCC 1402-1405: the Eucharist as the pledge of glory

CCC 611, 1366: institution of the priesthood at the Last Supper

Friday of the Passion of the Lord

CCC 602-618. 1992: the Passion of Christ

CCC 612, 2606, 2741: the prayer of Jesus

CCC 467, 540, 1137: Christ the High Priest

CCC 2825: Christ's obedience and ours

Easter Sunday of the Resurrection of the Lord

CCC 638-655, 989, 1001-1002: the Resurrection of Christ and our resurrection

CCC 647, 1167-1170, 1243, 1287: Easter, the Lord's Day

CCC 1212: the Sacraments of Initiation

CCC 1214-1222, 1226-1228, 1234-1245, 1254: Baptism

CCC 1286-1289: Confirmation

CCC 1322-1323: Eucharist

Second Sunday of Easter

CCC 448, 641-646: appearances of the risen Christ

CCC 1084-1089: sanctifying presence of the risen Christ in the liturgy

CCC 2177-2178, 1342: the Sunday Eucharist

CCC 654-655, 1988: our new birth in the Resurrection of Christ

CCC 976-983, 1441-1442: "I believe in the forgiveness of sins"

CCC 949-953, 1329, 1342, 2624, 2790: communion in spiritual goods

Third Sunday of Easter

CCC 1346-1347: the Eucharist and the experience of the disciples at Emmaus

CCC 642-644, 857, 995-996: the apostles and disciples as witnesses of the Resurrection

CCC 102, 601, 426-429, 2763: Christ the key to interpreting all Scripture

CCC 457, 604-605, 608, 615-616, 1476, 1992: Jesus, the Lamb offered for our sins

Fourth Sunday of Easter

CCC 754, 764, 2665: Christ the Shepherd and Gate

CCC 553, 857, 861, 881, 896, 1558, 1561, 1568, 1574: Pope and bishops as shepherds

CCC 874, 1120, 1465, 1536, 1548-1551, 1564, 2179, 2686: priests as shepherds

CCC 14, 189, 1064, 1226, 1236, 1253-1255, 1427-1429: conversion, faith, and baptism

CCC 618, 2447: Christ an example in bearing wrongs

Fifth Sunday of Easter

CCC 2746-2751: Christ's prayer at the Last Supper

CCC 661, 1025-1026, 2795: Christ opens for us the way to heaven

CCC 151, 1698, 2614, 2466: believing in Jesus

CCC 1569-1571: the order of deacons

CCC 782, 803, 1141, 1174, 1269, 1322: "a chosen race, a royal priesthood"

Sixth Sunday of Easter

CCC 2746-2751: Christ's prayer at the Last Supper
CCC 243, 388, 692, 729, 1433, 1848: the Holy Spirit as Advocate/Consoler
CCC 1083, 2670-2672: invoking the Holy Spirit

The Solemnity of the Ascension of the Lord

CCC 659-672, 697, 792, 965, 2795: the Ascension

Seventh Sunday of Easter: prayer and the spiritual life

CCC 2746-2751: Christ's prayer at the Last Supper
CCC 312, 434, 648, 664: the Father glorifies Christ
CCC 2614, 2741: Jesus prays for us
CCC 726, 2617-2619, 2673-2679: at prayer with Mary

The Solemnity of Pentecost

CCC 696, 726, 731-732, 737-741, 830, 1076, 1287, 2623: Pentecost
CCC 599, 597, 674, 715: apostolic witness on Pentecost
CCC 1152, 1226, 1302, 1556: the mystery of Pentecost continues in the Church
CCC 767, 775, 798, 796, 813, 1097, 1108-1109: the Church, communion in the Spirit

The Solemnity of the Most Holy Trinity

CCC 202, 232-260, 684, 732: the mystery of the Trinity
CCC 249, 813, 950, 1077-1109, 2845: the Trinity in the Church and her liturgy
CCC 2655, 2664-2672: the Trinity and prayer
CCC 2205: the family as an image of the Trinity

The Solemnity of the Most Holy Body and Blood of Christ

CCC 790, 1003, 1322-1419: the Holy Eucharist
CCC 805, 950, 2181-2182, 2637, 2845: the Eucharist and the communion of believers
CCC 1212, 1275, 1436, 2837: the Eucharist as spiritual food

The Solemnity of the Most Sacred Heart of Jesus

CCC 210-211, 604: God's mercy
CCC 430, 478, 545, 589, 1365, 1439, 1825, 1846: Christ's love for all
CCC 2669: the Heart of Christ worthy of adoration

CCC 766, 1225: the Church born from the pierced side of Christ

CCC 1432, 2100: Christ's love moves our hearts

Second Sunday in Ordinary Time

CCC 604-609: Jesus the Lamb of God who takes away sins of all

CCC 689-690: mission of Son and Holy Spirit

Third Sunday in Ordinary Time

CCC 551, 765: the call of the Twelve

CCC 541-543: Reign of God calls and gathers Jews and Gentiles

CCC 813-822: unity of the Church

Fourth Sunday in Ordinary Time

CCC 459, 520-521: Jesus a model of the beatitudes for followers

CCC 1716-1724: call to beatitude

CCC 64, 716: the poor and humble remnant bear hope of Messiah

Fifth Sunday in Ordinary Time

CCC 782: People of God to be salt and light

CCC 2044-2046: moral life and missionary witness

CCC 2443-2449: light on works of mercy, love for the poor

CCC 1243: the baptised (neophytes) are to be light of the world

CCC 272: Christ crucified is the wisdom of God

Sixth Sunday in Ordinary Time

CCC 577-582: Jesus and the Law

CCC 1961-1964 the old Law

CCC 2064-2068: the Decalogue in the tradition of the Church

Seventh Sunday in Ordinary Time

CCC 1933, 2303: love of neighbour incompatible with hatred of enemies

CCC 2262-2267: prohibition to harm others apart from self-defence

CCC 2842-2845: prayer and pardon of enemies

CCC 2012-2016: the heavenly Father's perfection calls all to holiness

CCC 1265: we become temples of the Holy Spirit in baptism

CCC 2684: saints are temples of the Holy Spirit

Eighth Sunday in Ordinary Time

CCC 302-314: divine providence and its role in history
CCC 2113-2115: idolatry subverts values; trust in providence vs. divination
CCC 2632: prayer of faithful petition for coming of the Kingdom
CCC 2830: trust in Providence does not mean idleness

Ninth Sunday in Ordinary Time

CCC 2822-2827: "Thy will be done"
CCC 2611: prayer is disposing heart to do God's will
CCC 1987-1995: justification

Tenth Sunday in Ordinary Time

CCC 545, 589: Jesus calls and pardons sinners
CCC 2099-2100: the sacrifice pleasing to God
CCC 144-146, 2572: Abraham a model of faith

Eleventh Sunday in Ordinary Time

CCC 551,761-766: the Church prefigured in Old Testament community
CCC 783-786: the Church a priestly, prophetic, royal people
CCC 849-865: the apostolic mission of the Church

Twelfth Sunday in Ordinary Time

CCC 852: the Spirit of Christ sustains the Christian mission
CCC 905: evangelising by the example of life
CCC 1808, 1816: courageous witness of faith overcomes fear and death
CCC 2471-2474: bear witness to the truth
CCC 359, 402-411, 615: Adam, Original Sin, Christ the New Adam

Thirteenth Sunday in Ordinary Time

CCC 2232-2233: to follow Christ is first vocation of Christian
CCC 537, 628, 790, 1213, 1226-1228, 1694: baptism, to die to self, to live for
Christ
CCC 1987: grace justifies through faith and baptism

Fourteenth Sunday in Ordinary Time

CCC 514-521: knowledge of mysteries of Christ, communion in his mysteries
CCC 238-242: the Father is revealed by the Son
CCC 989-990: the resurrection of the body

Fifteenth Sunday in Ordinary Time

CCC 546: Christ teaches through parables

CCC 1703-1709: capacity to know and correspond to the voice of God

CCC 2006-2011: God associates man in working of grace

CCC 1046-1047: creation part of the new universe

CCC 2707: the value of meditation

Sixteenth Sunday in Ordinary Time

CCC 543-550: the Kingdom of God

CCC 309-314: God's goodness and the scandal of evil

CCC 825, 827: weeds and seed of Gospel in everyone and in the Church

CCC 1425-1429: need for ongoing conversion

CCC 2630: prayer of petition voiced profoundly by the Holy Spirit

Seventeenth Sunday in Ordinary Time

CCC 407: cannot ignore wound of sin in discerning human situation

CCC 1777-1785: moral decision-making in rapport with God's will

CCC 1786-1789: seeking will of God in divine law in difficult circumstances

CCC 1038-1041: separation of good and evil at Judgement

CCC 1037: God predestines no one to hell

Eighteenth Sunday in Ordinary Time

CCC 2828-2837: give us this day our daily bread

CCC 1335: miracle of loaves prefigures the Eucharist

CCC 1391-1401: the fruits of Holy Communion

Nineteenth Sunday in Ordinary Time

CCC 164: faith experiences testing

CCC 272-274: only faith can follow mysterious ways of providence

CCC 671-672: in difficult times, cultivate trust that all is subject to Christ

CCC 56-64, 121-122, 218-219: history of covenants; God's love for Israel

CCC 839-840: the Church's relationship to the Jewish people

Twentieth Sunday in Ordinary Time

CCC 543-544: Kingdom first to Israel, now for all who believe

CCC 674: Christ's coming hope of Israel; their final acceptance of Messiah

CCC 2610: power of invocation with sincere faith

CCC 831, 849: the catholicity of the Church

Twenty-first Sunday in Ordinary Time

CCC 551-553: the Keys of the Kingdom

CCC 880-887: foundations of unity: the college of bishops with its head, the successor of Peter

Twenty-second Sunday in Ordinary Time

CCC 618: Christ calls his disciples to take up the Cross and follow him

CCC 555, 1460, 2100: the Cross as the way to Christ's glory

CCC 2015: way to perfection by way of the Cross

CCC 2427: carrying our cross in daily life

Twenty-third Sunday in Ordinary Time

CCC 2055: the Decalogue summed up in one command to love

CCC 1443-1445: reconciliation with the Church

CCC 2842-2845: "as we forgive those who trespass against us"

Twenty-fourth Sunday in Ordinary Time

CCC 218-221: God is love

CCC 294: God manifests his glory by sharing his goodness

CCC 2838-2845: "forgive us our trespasses"

Twenty-fifth Sunday in Ordinary Time

CCC 210-211: God of mercy and piety

CCC 588-589: Jesus identifies his compassion to sinners with God's

Twenty-sixth Sunday in Ordinary Time

CCC 1807: just person distinguished by habitual rectitude toward others

CCC 2842: only Holy Spirit can give us the mind of Christ

CCC 1928-1930, 2425-2426: the obligation of social justice

CCC 446-461: the Lordship of Christ

CCC 2822-2827: "Thy will be done"

Twenty-seventh Sunday in Ordinary Time

CCC 755: the Church as God's vineyard

CCC 1830-1832: gifts and fruits of the Holy Spirit

CCC 443: prophets are the servants, Christ is the Son

Twenty-eighth Sunday in Ordinary Time

CCC 543-546: Jesus invites sinners, but demands conversion
CCC 1402-1405, 2837: the Eucharist is the foretaste of the Messianic Banquet

Twenty-ninth Sunday in Ordinary Time

CCC 1897-1917: participation in the social sphere
CCC 2238-2244: duties of citizens

Thirtieth Sunday in Ordinary Time

CCC 2052-2074: the Ten Commandments interpreted through twofold love
CCC 2061-2063: moral life a response to the Lord's initiative of love

Thirty-first Sunday in Ordinary Time

CCC 2044: moral life and Christian witness
CCC 876, 1550-1551: priesthood for service; human frailty of leaders

Thirty-second Sunday in Ordinary Time

CCC 671-672: we wait for all to be made subject to Christ
CCC 988-991: the just will live forever with the risen Christ
CCC 1036, 2612: vigilant waiting for the Lord's return

Thirty-third Sunday in Ordinary Time

CCC 2006-2011: our merits for good works come from God's goodness
CCC 1038-1041: our works manifested at the Last Judgement
CCC 1048-1050: keeping busy as we await the Lord's return
CCC 1936-1937: diversity of talents
CCC 2331, 2334: dignity of woman
CCC 1603-1605: marriage in the order of creation

Solemnity of Christ the King: Christ the origin and goal of history

CCC 440, 446-451, 668-672, 783, 786, 908, 2105, 2628: Christ as Lord and King
CCC 678-679, 1001, 1038-1041: Christ as Judge
CCC 2816-2821: "Thy Kingdom Come"

CYCLE B

First Sunday of Advent

CCC 668-677, 769: the final tribulation and Christ's return in glory
CCC 451, 671, 1130, 1403, 2817: "Come, Lord Jesus!"
CCC 35: God gives humanity grace to accept Revelation, welcome the Messiah
CCC 827, 1431, 2677, 2839: acknowledging that we are sinners

Second Sunday of Advent

CCC 522, 711-716, 722: the prophets and the expectation of the Messiah
CCC 523, 717-720: the mission of John the Baptist
CCC 1042-1050: a new heaven and a new earth

Third Sunday of Advent

CCC 30, 163, 301, 736, 1829, 1832, 2015, 2362: joy
CCC 713-714: characteristics of the awaited Messiah
CCC 218-219: God's love for Israel
CCC 772, 796: the Church as the Bride of Christ

Fourth Sunday of Advent

CCC 484-494: the Annunciation
CCC 439, 496, 559, 2616: Jesus is the Son of David
CCC 143-149, 494, 2087: the "obedience of faith"

The Solemnity of Christmas

CCC 456-460, 466: "Why did the Word become flesh?"
CCC 461-463, 470-478: the Incarnation
CCC 437, 525-526: the Christmas mystery
CCC 439, 496, 559, 2616: Jesus is the Son of David
CCC 65, 102: God has said everything in his Word
CCC 333: the incarnate Christ worshipped by the angels
CCC 1159-1162, 2131, 2502: the Incarnation and images of Christ

The Holy Family

CCC 531-534: the Holy Family
CCC 1655-1658, 2204-2206: the Christian family, a domestic Church
CCC 2214-2233: duties of family members

CCC 529, 583, 695: the Presentation in the Temple

CCC 144-146, 165, 489, 2572, 2676: Abraham and Sarah as models of faith

The Solemnity of Mary, the Mother of God

CCC 464-469: Jesus Christ, true God and true Man

CCC 495, 2677: Mary is the Mother of God

CCC 1, 52, 270, 294, 422, 654, 1709, 2009: our adoption as sons

CCC 527, 577-582: Jesus submits to the Law, and perfects it

CCC 580, 1972: the New Law frees from restrictions of the Old Law

CCC 683, 689, 1695, 2766, 2777-2778: in the Holy Spirit we can call God "Abba"

CCC 430-435, 2666-2668, 2812: the name of Jesus

Second Sunday after the Nativity

CCC 151, 241, 291, 423, 445, 456-463, 504-505, 526, 1216, 2466, 2787: John's Prologue

CCC 272, 295, 299, 474, 721, 1831: Christ the Wisdom of God

CCC 158, 283, 1303, 1831, 2500: God gives us wisdom

Solemnity of the Epiphany

CCC 528, 724: the Epiphany

CCC 280, 529, 748, 1165, 2466, 2715: Christ the light of the nations

CCC 60, 442, 674, 755, 767, 774-776, 781, 831: the Church, sacrament of human unity

First Sunday of Lent

CCC 394, 538-540, 2119: the temptation of Jesus

CCC 2846-2849: "Lead us not into temptation"

CCC 56-58, 71: the Covenant with Noah

CCC 845, 1094, 1219: Noah's Ark prefigures the Church and baptism

CCC 1116, 1129, 1222: Covenant and sacraments (especially baptism)

CCC 1257, 1811: God saves through baptism

Second Sunday of Lent

CCC 554-556. 568: the Transfiguration

CCC 59, 145-146, 2570-2572: the obedience of Abraham

CCC 153-159: characteristics of faith

CCC 2059: God manifests his glory to make known his will

CCC 603, 1373, 2634, 2852: Christ is for us

Third Sunday of Lent

CCC 459, 577-582: Jesus and the Law

CCC 593, 583-586: Temple prefigures Christ; he is the Temple

CCC 1967-1968: the New Law completes the Old

CCC 272, 550, 853: Christ's power revealed in the Cross

Fourth Sunday of Lent

CCC 389, 457-458, 846, 1019, 1507: Christ as Saviour

CCC 679: Christ the Lord of eternal life

CCC 55: God wants to give man eternal life

CCC 710: Israel's exile foreshadowed the Passion

Fifth Sunday of Lent

CCC 606-607: Christ's life an offering to the Father

CCC 542, 607: Christ's desire to give his life for our salvation

CCC 690, 729: the Spirit glorifies the Son, the Son glorifies the Father

CCC 662, 2853: Christ ascended in glory as our victory

CCC 56-64, 220, 715, 762, 1965: the history of the covenants

Palm Sunday of the Lord's Passion

CCC 557-560: Christ's entry into Jerusalem

CCC 602-618: the Passion of Christ

CCC 2816: Christ's kingship gained through his death and Resurrection

CCC 654, 1067-1068, 1085, 1362: the Paschal Mystery and the liturgy

Thursday of the Lord's Supper

CCC 1337-1344: the institution of the Eucharist

CCC 1359-1361: Eucharist as thanksgiving

CCC 610, 1362-1372, 1382, 1436: Eucharist as sacrifice

CCC 1373-1381: the real presence of Christ in the Eucharist

CCC 1384-1401, 2837: Holy Communion

CCC 1402-1405: the Eucharist as the pledge of glory

CCC 611, 1366: institution of the priesthood at the Last Supper

Friday of the Passion of the Lord

CCC 602-618. 1992: the Passion of Christ

CCC 612, 2606, 2741: the prayer of Jesus

CCC 467, 540, 1137: Christ the High Priest
CCC 2825: Christ's obedience and ours

Easter Sunday of the Resurrection of the Lord

CCC 638-655, 989, 1001-1002: the Resurrection of Christ and our resurrection
CCC 647, 1167-1170, 1243, 1287: Easter, the Lord's Day
CCC 1212: the Sacraments of Initiation
CCC 1214-1222, 1226-1228, 1234-1245, 1254: Baptism
CCC 1286-1289: Confirmation
CCC 1322-1323: Eucharist

Second Sunday of Easter

CCC 448, 641-646: appearances of the risen Christ
CCC 1084-1089: sanctifying presence of the risen Christ in the liturgy
CCC 2177-2178, 1342: the Sunday Eucharist
CCC 654-655, 1988: our new birth in the Resurrection of Christ
CCC 976-983, 1441-1442: "I believe in the forgiveness of sins"
CCC 949-953, 1329, 1342, 2624, 2790: communion in spiritual goods

Third Sunday of Easter

CCC 1346-1347: the Eucharist and the experience of the disciples at Emmaus
CCC 642-644, 857, 995-996: the apostles and disciples as witnesses of the Resurrection
CCC 102, 601, 426-429, 2763: Christ the key to interpreting all Scripture
CCC 519, 662, 1137: Christ, our Advocate in heaven

Fourth Sunday of Easter

CCC 754, 764, 2665: Christ the Shepherd and Gate
CCC 553, 857, 861, 881, 896, 1558, 1561, 1568, 1574: Pope and bishops as shepherds
CCC 874, 1120, 1465, 1536, 1548-1551, 1564, 2179, 2686: priests as shepherds
CCC 756: Christ the cornerstone
CCC 1, 104, 239, 1692, 1709, 2009, 2736: we are God's children now

Fifth Sunday of Easter

CCC 2746-2751: Christ's prayer at the Last Supper
CCC 736-737, 755, 787, 1108, 1988, 2074: Christ is the vine, we are the branches
CCC 953, 1822-1829: charity

Sixth Sunday of Easter

CCC 2746-2751: Christ's prayer at the Last Supper

CCC 214, 218-221, 231, 257, 733, 2331, 2577: God is love

CCC 1789, 1822-1829, 2067, 2069: love of God and neighbour fulfils the Commandments

CCC 2347, 2709: friendship with Christ

The Solemnity of the Ascension of the Lord

CCC 659-672, 697, 792, 965, 2795: the Ascension

Seventh Sunday of Easter

CCC 2746-2751: Christ's prayer at the Last Supper

CCC 2614, 2741: Jesus prays for us

CCC 611, 2812, 2821: Jesus's prayer sanctifies us, especially in the Eucharist

The Solemnity of Pentecost

CCC 696, 726, 731-732, 737-741, 830, 1076, 1287, 2623: Pentecost

CCC 599, 597,674, 715: apostolic witness on Pentecost

CCC 1152, 1226, 1302, 1556: the mystery of Pentecost continues in the Church

CCC 767, 775, 798, 796, 813, 1097, 1108-1109: the Church, communion in the Spirit

The Solemnity of the Most Holy Trinity

CCC 202, 232-260, 684, 732: the mystery of the Trinity

CCC 249, 813, 950, 1077-1109, 2845: the Trinity in the Church and her liturgy

CCC 2655, 2664-2672: the Trinity and prayer

CCC 2205: the family as an image of the Trinity

The Solemnity of the Most Holy Body and Blood of Christ

CCC 790, 1003, 1322-1419: the Holy Eucharist

CCC 805, 950, 2181-2182, 2637, 2845: the Eucharist and the communion of believers

CCC 1212, 1275, 1436, 2837: the Eucharist as spiritual food

The Solemnity of the Most Sacred Heart of Jesus

CCC 210-211, 604: God's mercy

CCC 430, 478, 545, 589, 1365, 1439, 1825, 1846: Christ's love for all

CCC 2669: the Heart of Christ worthy of adoration

CCC 766, 1225: the Church born from the pierced side of Christ
CCC 1432, 2100: Christ's love moves our hearts

Second Sunday in Ordinary Time

CCC 462, 516, 2568, 2824: the Father's will fulfilled in Christ
CCC 543-546: to welcome the Kingdom, welcome the Word of God
CCC 873-874: Christ the source of Christian vocation
CCC 364, 1004: the dignity of the body
CCC 1656, 2226: helping children discover their vocation

Third Sunday in Ordinary Time

CCC 51-64: God's plan of Revelation
CCC 1427-1433: inner, ongoing conversion
CCC 1886-1889: conversion and society

Fourth Sunday in Ordinary Time

CCC 547-550: Jesus accompanies words with miracles
CCC 447, 438, 550: Jesus's power over demons
CCC 64, 762, 2595: the role of the prophet
CCC 922, 1618-1620: virginity for the sake of the Kingdom

Fifth Sunday in Ordinary Time

CCC 547-550: healing as a sign of messianic times
CCC 1502-1505: Christ the Healer
CCC 875, 1122: the urgency of preaching

Sixth Sunday in Ordinary Time

CCC 1474: living in Christ unites all believers in him
CCC 1939-1942: human solidarity
CCC 2288-2291: respect for health

Seventh Sunday in Ordinary Time

CCC 1421, 1441-1442: Christ the healer of soul and body
CCC 987, 1441, 1741: Christ forgives sins
CCC 1425-1426: reconciliation after baptism
CCC 1065: Christ our "Amen"

Eighth Sunday in Ordinary Time

CCC 772-773, 796: the Church, the mystery of union with God
CCC 796: the Church as the Bride of Christ

Ninth Sunday in Ordinary Time

CCC 345-349, 582, 2168-2173: the Lord's Day
CCC 1005-1014, 1470, 1681-1683: dying and living in Christ

Tenth Sunday in Ordinary Time

CCC 410-412: the Protoevangelium
CCC 374-379: man in paradise
CCC 385-409: the fall
CCC 517, 550: Christ as exorcist

Eleventh Sunday in Ordinary Time

CCC 543-546: announcing the Kingdom of God
CCC 2653-2654, 2660, 2716: the Kingdom grows by hearing the Word

Twelfth Sunday in Ordinary Time

CCC 423, 464-469: Jesus, true God and true Man
CCC 1814-1816: faith as gift of God, and human response
CCC 671-672: maintaining faith in adversity

Thirteenth Sunday in Ordinary Time

CCC 548-549, 646, 994: Jesus raises the dead
CCC 1009-1014: death transformed by Christ
CCC 1042-1050: hope for a new heaven and a new earth

Fourteenth Sunday in Ordinary Time

CCC 2581-2584: prophets and conversion of heart
CCC 436: Christ as prophet
CCC 162: perseverance in faith
CCC 268, 273, 1508: power is made perfect in weakness

Fifteenth Sunday in Ordinary Time

CCC 1506-1509: disciples share in Christ's healing mission
CCC737-741: Church called to proclaim and bear witness
CCC 849-856: origin and scope of the Church's mission
CCC 1122, 1533: mission-mindedness

CCC 693, 698, 706, 1107, 1296: the Holy Spirit as God's guarantee and seal

CCC 492: Mary as a unique example of being chosen before the foundation of the world

Sixteenth Sunday in Ordinary Time

CCC 2302-2306: Christ our peace

CCC 2437-2442: witnesses and workers for peace and justice

Seventeenth Sunday in Ordinary Time

CCC 1335: the miracle of the loaves and fishes prefigures the Eucharist

CCC 814-815, 949-959: sharing of gifts in the communion of the Church

Eighteenth Sunday in Ordinary Time

CCC 1333-1336: Eucharistic signs of bread and wine

CCC 1691-1696: life in Christ

Nineteenth Sunday in Ordinary Time

CCC 1341-1344: "Do this in memory of me"

CCC 1384-1390: take and eat: Communion

Twentieth Sunday in Ordinary Time

CCC 1402-1405: the Eucharist, pledge of future glory

CCC 2828-2837: the Eucharist is our daily bread

CCC 1336: scandal

Twenty-first Sunday in Ordinary Time

CCC 796: the Church as the Bride of Christ

CCC 1061-1065: God's utter fidelity and love

CCC 1612-1617, 2360-2365: marriage in the Lord

Twenty-second Sunday in Ordinary Time

CCC577-582: Christ and the Law

CCC 1961-1974: the Old Law and the Gospel

Twenty-third Sunday in Ordinary Time

CCC 1503-1505: Christ the Physician

CCC 1151-1152: signs used by Christ; sacramental signs

CCC 270-271: the mercy of God

Twenty-fourth Sunday in Ordinary Time

CCC 713-716: the path of the Messiah traced out in the "Servant Songs"
CCC 440, 571-572, 601: Jesus suffered and died for our salvation
CCC 618: our participation in Christ's sacrifice
CCC 2044-2046: good works manifest faith

Twenty-fifth Sunday in Ordinary Time

CCC 539, 565, 600-605, 713: Christ, obedient Servant of God
CCC 786: to serve is to reign
CCC 1547, 1551: priestly ministry as service
CCC 2538-2540: the sin of envy
CCC 2302-2306: safeguarding peace

Twenty-sixth Sunday in Ordinary Time

CCC 821, 1126, 1636: ecumenical dialogue
CCC 2445-2446, 2536, 2544-2547: the danger of immoderate riches
CCC 1852: jealousy

Twenty-seventh Sunday in Ordinary Time

CCC 1602-1617, 1643-1651, 2331-2336: conjugal fidelity
CCC 2331-2336: divorce
CCC 1832: fidelity, a fruit of Spirit
CCC 2044, 2147, 2156, 2223, 2787: the fidelity of the baptised

Twenty-eighth Sunday in Ordinary Time

CCC 101-104: Christ, unique Word of Scripture
CCC 131-133: Scripture in life of the Church
CCC 2653-2654: Scripture as a fountain of prayer
CCC 1723, 2536, 2444-2447: poverty of heart

Twenty-ninth Sunday in Ordinary Time

CCC 599-609: Christ's redemptive death in the plan of salvation
CCC 520: Christ's self-emptying as an example for us to imitate
CCC 467, 540, 1137: Christ the High Priest

Thirtieth Sunday in Ordinary Time

CCC 547-550: Jesus performed messianic signs
CCC 1814-1816: faith, a gift of God
CCC 2734-2737: filial confidence in prayer

Thirty-first Sunday in Ordinary Time

CCC 2083: commandments as a call for a response of love
CCC 2052, 2093-2094: the first commandment
CCC 1539-1547: holy orders in the economy of salvation

Thirty-second Sunday in Ordinary Time

CCC 519-521: Christ gave his life for us
CCC 2544-2547: poverty of heart
CCC 1434, 1438, 1753, 1969, 2447: almsgiving
CCC 2581-2584: Elijah and conversion of heart
CCC 1021-1022: the particular judgement

Thirty-third Sunday in Ordinary Time

CCC1038-1050: the Last Judgement; hope of a new heaven and a new earth
CCC 613-614, 1365-1367: Christ's one perfect sacrifice and the Eucharist

Solemnity of Christ the King: Christ the origin and goal of history

CCC 440, 446-451, 668-672, 783, 786, 908, 2105, 2628: Christ as Lord and King
CCC 678-679, 1001, 1038-1041: Christ as Judge
CCC 2816-2821: "Thy Kingdom Come"

CYCLE C

First Sunday of Advent

CCC 668-677, 769: the final tribulation and Christ's return in glory
CCC 451, 671, 1130, 1403, 2817: "Come, Lord Jesus!"
CCC 439, 496, 559, 2616: Jesus is the Son of David
CCC 207, 210-214, 270, 1062-1063: God is faithful and merciful

Second Sunday of Advent

CCC 522, 711-716, 722: the prophets and the expectation of the Messiah
CCC 523, 717-720: the mission of John the Baptist
CCC 710: Israel's exile foreshadowed the Passion
CCC 2532, 2636: Paul's solicitude

Third Sunday of Advent

CCC 30, 163, 301, 736, 1829, 1832, 2015, 2362: joy
CCC 523-524, 535: John prepares the way for the Messiah
CCC 430-435: Jesus the Saviour

Fourth Sunday of Advent

CCC 148, 495, 717, 2676: the Visitation
CCC 462, 606-607, 2568, 2824: the Son becomes incarnate to do the Father's will

The Solemnity of Christmas

CCC 456-460, 466: "Why did the Word become flesh?"
CCC 461-463, 470-478: the Incarnation
CCC 437, 525-526: the Christmas mystery
CCC 439, 496, 559, 2616: Jesus is the Son of David
CCC 65, 102: God has said everything in his Word
CCC 333: the incarnate Christ worshipped by the angels
CCC 1159-1162, 2131, 2502: the Incarnation and images of Christ

The Holy Family

CCC 531-534: the Holy Family
CCC 1655-1658, 2204-2206: the Christian family, a domestic Church
CCC 2214-2233: duties of family members

CCC 534, 583, 2599: the Finding in the Temple

CCC 64, 489, 2578: Hannah and Samuel

CCC 1, 104, 239, 1692, 1709, 2009, 2736: we are God's children now

CCC 163, 1023, 1161, 2519, 2772: we shall see him face to face and be like him

The Solemnity of Mary, the Mother of God

CCC 464-469: Jesus Christ, true God and true Man

CCC 495, 2677: Mary is the Mother of God

CCC 1, 52, 270, 294, 422, 654, 1709, 2009: our adoption as sons

CCC 527, 577-582: Jesus submits to the Law, and perfects it

CCC 580, 1972: the New Law frees from restrictions of the Old Law

CCC 683, 689, 1695, 2766, 2777-2778: in Holy Spirit we can call God "Abba"

CCC 430-435, 2666-2668, 2812: the name of Jesus

Second Sunday after the Nativity

CCC 151, 241, 291, 423, 445, 456-463, 504-505, 526, 1216, 2466, 2787: John's Prologue

CCC 272, 295, 299, 474, 721, 1831: Christ the Wisdom of God

CCC 158, 283, 1303, 1831, 2500: God gives us wisdom

Solemnity of the Epiphany

CCC 528, 724: the Epiphany

CCC 280, 529, 748, 1165, 2466, 2715: Christ the light of the nations

CCC 60, 442, 674, 755, 767, 774-776, 781, 831: the Church, sacrament of human unity

First Sunday of Lent

CCC 394, 538-540, 2119: the temptation of Jesus

CCC 2846-2849: "Lead us not into temptation"

CCC 1505: Christ frees from evil

CCC 142-143, 309: faith as submission to God, response to God, answer to evil

CCC 59-63: God forms his priestly people through Abraham and the Exodus

Second Sunday of Lent

CCC 554-556. 568: the Transfiguration

CCC 59, 145-146, 2570-2572: the obedience of Abraham

CCC 1000: faith opens the way to comprehending the mystery of the Resurrection

CCC 645, 999-1001: the resurrection of the body

Third Sunday of Lent

CCC 210, 2575-2577: God calls Moses, hears prayers of his people

CCC 1963-1964: observance of Law prepares for conversion

CCC 2851: evil and its works as obstacle on way of salvation

CCC 128-130, 1094: Old Testament "types" fulfilled in New

CCC 736, 1108-1109, 1129, 1521, 1724, 1852, 2074, 2516, 2345, 2731: bearing fruit

Fourth Sunday of Lent

CCC 1439, 1465, 1481, 1700, 2839: the prodigal son

CCC 207, 212, 214: God is faithful to his promises

CCC 1441, 1443: God pardons sin and restores the sinner to the community

CCC 982: the door of pardon is open to all who repent

CCC 1334: Israel's daily bread was the fruit of the promised land

Fifth Sunday of Lent

CCC 430, 545, 589, 1846-1847: Jesus manifests the Father's mercy

CCC 133, 428, 648, 989, 1006: the surpassing wealth of knowing Christ

CCC 2475-2479: rash judgement

Palm Sunday of the Lord's Passion

CCC 557-560: Christ's entry into Jerusalem

CCC 602-618: the Passion of Christ

CCC 2816: Christ's kingship gained through his death and Resurrection

CCC 654, 1067-1068, 1085, 1362: the Paschal Mystery and the liturgy

Thursday of the Lord's Supper

CCC 1337-1344: the institution of the Eucharist

CCC 1359-1361: Eucharist as thanksgiving

CCC 610, 1362-1372, 1382, 1436: Eucharist as sacrifice

CCC 1373-1381: the real presence of Christ in the Eucharist

CCC 1384-1401, 2837: Holy Communion

CCC 1402-1405: the Eucharist as the pledge of glory

CCC 611, 1366: the institution of the priesthood at the Last Supper

Friday of the Passion of the Lord

CCC 602-618. 1992: the Passion of Christ
CCC 612, 2606, 2741: the prayer of Jesus
CCC 467, 540, 1137: Christ the High Priest
CCC 2825: Christ's obedience and ours

Easter Sunday of the Resurrection of the Lord

CCC 638-655, 989, 1001-1002: the Resurrection of Christ and our resurrection
CCC 647, 1167-1170, 1243, 1287: Easter, the Lord's Day
CCC 1212: the Sacraments of Initiation
CCC 1214-1222, 1226-1228, 1234-1245, 1254: Baptism
CCC 1286-1289: Confirmation
CCC 1322-1323: Eucharist

Second Sunday of Easter

CCC 448, 641-646: appearances of the risen Christ
CCC 1084-1089: the sanctifying presence of the risen Christ in the liturgy
CCC 2177-2178, 1342: the Sunday Eucharist
CCC 654-655, 1988: our new birth in the Resurrection of Christ
CCC 976-983, 1441-1442: "I believe in the forgiveness of sins"
CCC 949-953, 1329, 1342, 2624, 2790: communion in spiritual goods
CCC 612, 625, 635, 2854: Christ the "Living One" holds the keys of death

Third Sunday of Easter

CCC 642-644, 857, 995-996: the apostles and disciples as witnesses of the Resurrection
CCC 553, 641, 881, 1429: the risen Christ and Peter
CCC 1090, 1137-1139, 1326: the heavenly liturgy

Fourth Sunday of Easter

CCC 754, 764, 2665: Christ the Shepherd and Gate
CCC 553, 857, 861, 881, 896, 1558, 1561, 1568, 1574: Pope and bishops as shepherds
CCC 874, 1120, 1465, 1536, 1548-1551, 1564, 2179, 2686: priests as shepherds
CCC 60, 442, 543, 674, 724, 755, 775, 781: the Church is made up of Jews and Gentiles
CCC 957, 1138, 1173, 2473-2474: our communion with the martyrs

Fifth Sunday of Easter

CCC 2746-2751: Christ's prayer at the Last Supper
CCC 459, 1823, 2074, 2196, 2822, 2842: "as I have loved you"
CCC 756, 865, 1042-1050, 2016, 2817: a new heaven and a new earth

Sixth Sunday of Easter

CCC 2746-2751: Christ's prayer at the Last Supper
CCC 243, 388, 692, 729, 1433, 1848: the Holy Spirit as Advocate/Consoler
CCC 1965-1974: the New Law fulfills the Old
CCC 865, 869, 1045, 1090, 1198, 2016: the heavenly Jerusalem

The Solemnity of the Ascension of the Lord

CCC 659-672, 697, 792, 965, 2795: the Ascension

Seventh Sunday of Easter

CCC 521: through Christ we live in communion with Father
CCC 787-790, 795, 1044-1047: the Church is communion with and in Christ

The Solemnity of Pentecost

CCC 696, 726, 731-732, 737-741, 830, 1076, 1287, 2623: Pentecost
CCC 599, 597,674, 715: apostolic witness on Pentecost
CCC 1152, 1226, 1302, 1556: the mystery of Pentecost continues in the Church
CCC 767, 775, 798, 796, 813, 1097, 1108-1109: the Church, communion in the Spirit

The Solemnity of the Most Holy Trinity

CCC 202, 232-260, 684, 732: the mystery of the Trinity
CCC 249, 813, 950, 1077-1109, 2845: the Trinity in the Church and her liturgy
CCC 2655, 2664-2672: the Trinity and prayer
CCC 2205: the family as an image of the Trinity

The Solemnity of the Most Holy Body and Blood of Christ

CCC 790, 1003, 1322-1419: the Holy Eucharist
CCC 805, 950, 2181-2182, 2637, 2845: the Eucharist and the communion of believers
CCC 1212, 1275, 1436, 2837: the Eucharist as spiritual food

The Solemnity of the Most Sacred Heart of Jesus

CCC 210-211, 604: God's mercy
CCC 430, 478, 545, 589, 1365, 1439, 1825, 1846: Christ's love for all
CCC 2669: the Heart of Christ worthy of adoration
CCC 766, 1225: the Church born from the pierced side of Christ
CCC 1432, 2100: Christ's love moves our hearts

Second Sunday in Ordinary Time

CCC 528: at Cana, Christ shows himself to be Messiah, Son of God, Saviour
CCC 796: the Church as Bride of Christ
CCC 1612-1617: marriage in the Lord
CCC 2618: Mary's intercession at Cana
CCC 799-801, 951, 2003: charisms at the service of the Church

Third Sunday in Ordinary Time

CCC 714: Old Testament expectation of the Messiah and the Spirit
CCC 1965-1974: new Law and Gospel
CCC 106, 108, 515: God inspires human authors of Scripture, and readers
CCC 787-795: the Church as the Body of Christ

Fourth Sunday in Ordinary Time

CCC 436, 1241, 1546: Christ as prophet
CCC 904-907: our participation in Christ's prophetic office
CCC 103-104: faith, the beginning of eternal life
CCC 1822-1829: charity
CCC 772-773, 953: communion in the Church
CCC 314, 1023, 2519: those in heaven behold God face to face

Fifth Sunday in Ordinary Time

CCC 520, 618, 923, 1618, 1642, 2053: all are called to follow Christ
CCC 2144, 2732: awe in God's presence vs. presumption
CCC 631-644: the Apostles as witnesses of the Resurrection

Sixth Sunday in Ordinary Time

CCC 1820: Christian hope begins in the giving of the Beatitudes
CCC 2544-2547: poverty of heart; the Lord grieves over the rich
CCC 655, 989-991, 1002-1003: hope in the Resurrection

Seventh Sunday in Ordinary Time

CCC 210-211: God of mercy
CCC 1825, 1935, 1968, 2303, 2647, 2842-2845: forgiveness of enemies
CCC 359, 504: Christ as the New Adam

Eighth Sunday in Ordinary Time

CCC 2563: the heart is the home of truth
CCC 1755-1756: good acts and evil acts
CCC 1783-1794: forming conscience and decision-making
CCC 2690: spiritual direction
CCC 1009-1013: Christian view of death

Ninth Sunday in Ordinary Time

CCC 543-546: all are called to enter Kingdom of God
CCC 774-776: the Church as universal sacrament of salvation
CCC 2580: Solomon's prayer at the dedication of the Temple
CCC 583-586: Jesus and the Temple

Tenth Sunday in Ordinary Time

CCC 646, 994: in raising the dead Christ announces his own Resurrection
CCC 1681: Christian meaning of death associated with the Resurrection
CCC 2583: Elijah and the widow
CCC 2637: Christ frees creation from sin and death

Eleventh Sunday in Ordinary Time

CCC 1441-1442: only God forgives sin
CCC 1987-1995: justification
CCC 2517-1519: purification of heart
CCC 1481, 1736, 2538: David and Nathan

Twelfth Sunday in Ordinary Time

CCC 599-605: Christ's redemptive death in the plan of salvation
CCC 1435: take up the cross daily and follow Christ
CCC 787-791: Church is communion with Christ
CCC 1425, 1227, 1243, 2348: "putting on" Christ; baptism and chastity

Thirteenth Sunday in Ordinary Time

CCC 587: Jesus's ascent to Jerusalem for his death and Resurrection
CCC 2052-2055: Master, what must I do...?
CCC 1036, 1816: the urgency of discipleship

Fourteenth Sunday in Ordinary Time

CCC 541-546: the Kingdom of God is at hand
CCC 787, 858-859: the Apostles, united to the mission of Christ
CCC 2122: "the labourer deserves his food"
CCC 2816-2821: "Your kingdom come"
CCC 555, 1816, 2015: the Cross as the way to follow Christ

Fifteenth Sunday in Ordinary Time

CCC 299, 381: man created in the image of God; the first-born
CCC 1931-1933: viewing neighbour as another self
CCC 2447: corporal works of mercy
CCC 1465: the priest as Good Samaritan in the sacrament of Penance
CCC 203, 291, 331, 703: the Word and creation, visible and invisible

Sixteenth Sunday in Ordinary Time

CCC 2571: Abraham's hospitality
CCC 2241: welcome the stranger
CCC 2709-2719: contemplation
CCC 618, 1508: sharing in Christ's sufferings for his Body
CCC 568, 772: "the hope of glory" in the Church and in her sacraments

Seventeenth Sunday in Ordinary Time

CCC 2634-2636: prayer of intercession
CCC 2566-2567: universal call to prayer
CCC 2761-2772: the Lord's Prayer as a synthesis of Gospel
CCC 2609-2610, 2613, 2777-2785: turning to God with persistence and filial trust
CCC 2654: *lectio divina*
CCC 537, 628, 1002, 1227: buried and risen in baptism

Eighteenth Sunday in Ordinary Time

CCC 661, 1042-1050, 1821: hope for a new heaven and a new earth
CCC 2535-2540, 2547, 2728: the disorder of covetousness

Nineteenth Sunday in Ordinary Time

CCC 144-149: the obedience of faith
CCC 1817-1821: the virtue of hope
CCC 2729-2733: prayer as humble vigilance of heart
CCC 144-146, 165, 2572, 2676: Abraham, a model of faith

Twentieth Sunday in Ordinary Time

CCC 575-576: Christ, a sign of contradiction
CCC 1816: a disciple should witness to the faith with boldness
CCC 2471-2474: giving testimony to the truth
CCC 946-957, 1370, 2683-2684: our communion with the saints
CCC 1161: sacred images remind us of the "cloud of witnesses"

Twenty-first Sunday in Ordinary Time

CCC 543-546: all called to enter the Kingdom
CCC 774-776: the Church as universal sacrament of salvation
CCC 2825-2827: do the Father's will to enter the Kingdom
CCC 853, 1036, 1344, 1889, 2656: the narrow way

Twenty-second Sunday in Ordinary Time

CCC 525-526: the Incarnation as a mystery of humility
CCC 2535-2540: the disorder of concupiscence
CCC 2546, 2559, 2631, 2713: prayer calls for humility and poverty of spirit
CCC 1090, 1137-1139: our participation in the heavenly liturgy
CCC 2188: Sunday lets us share in the festal assembly of heaven

Twenty-third Sunday in Ordinary Time

CCC 273, 300, 314: God's transcendence
CCC 36-43: knowledge of God according to the Church
CCC 2544: prefer Christ to all else
CCC 914-919, 931-932: following Christ in consecrated life

Twenty-fourth Sunday in Ordinary Time

CCC 210-211: God of mercy
CCC 604-605, 1846-1848: God takes the initiative in redemption
CCC 1439, 1700, 2839: the Prodigal Son as an example of conversion
CCC 1465, 1481: the Prodigal Son and the sacrament of Penance

Twenty-fifth Sunday in Ordinary Time

> CCC 2407-2414: respect for the property of others
> CCC 2443-2449: love for the poor
> CCC 2635: pray for others' interest, not just for one's own
> CCC 65-67, 480, 667: Christ our one Mediator
> CCC 2113, 2424, 2848: no one can serve two masters
> CCC 1900, 2636: intercession for rulers

Twenty-sixth Sunday in Ordinary Time

> CCC 1939-1942: human solidarity
> CCC 2437-2449: solidarity among nations; love for poor
> CCC 2831: hunger in world; solidarity; prayer
> CCC 633, 1021, 2463, 2831: Lazarus
> CCC 1033-1037: Hell

Twenty-seventh Sunday in Ordinary Time

> CCC 153-165, 2087-2089: faith
> CCC 84: the deposit of faith given to Church
> CCC 91-93: the supernatural sense of faith

Twenty-eighth Sunday in Ordinary Time

> CCC 1503-1505, 2616: Christ the healer
> CCC 543-550, 1151: signs of the Kingdom of God
> CCC 224, 2637-2638: thanksgiving
> CCC 1010: the Christian meaning of death

Twenty-ninth Sunday in Ordinary Time

> CCC 2574-2577: Moses and prayer of intercession
> CCC 2629-2633: prayer of petition
> CCC 2653-2654: the Word of God, a source of prayer
> CCC 2816-2821: "Thy kingdom come"
> CCC 875: urgency of the preaching task

Thirtieth Sunday in Ordinary Time

> CCC 588, 2559, 2613, 2631: humility as the foundation of prayer
> CCC 2616: Jesus hears prayer made in faith
> CCC 2628: adoration as the attitude of man who knows he is a creature
> CCC 2631: prayer for pardon as the first kind of prayer of petition

Thirty-first Sunday in Ordinary Time

> CCC 293-294, 299, 341, 353: the universe created for God's glory
> CCC 1459, 2412, 2487: reparation

Thirty-second Sunday in Ordinary Time

> CCC 992-996: the progressive revelation of resurrection
> CCC 997-1004: our resurrection in Christ
> CCC 1023-1029: heaven
> CCC 1030-1032: purgatory, the final purification

Thirty-third Sunday in Ordinary Time

> CCC 162-165: perseverance in faith; faith as the beginning of eternal life
> CCC 675-677: the final trial of the Church
> CCC 307, 531, 2427-2429: human labour as redemptive
> CCC 673, 1001, 2730: the last day

Solemnity of Christ the King: Christ the origin and goal of history

> CCC 440, 446-451, 668-672, 783, 786, 908, 2105, 2628: Christ as Lord and King
> CCC 678-679, 1001, 1038-1041: Christ as Judge
> CCC 2816-2821: "Thy Kingdom Come"

OTHER HOLY DAYS (CCC 2177)

March 19: The Solemnity of Saint Joseph

CCC 437, 497, 532-534, 1014, 1846, 2177: Saint Joseph
CCC 2214-2220: duties of children to their parents

June 29: The Solemnity of the Apostles Peter and Paul

CCC 153, 424, 440, 442, 552, 765, 880-881: Saint Peter
CCC 442, 601, 639, 642, 1508, 2632-2633, 2636, 2638: Saint Paul

August 15: The Solemnity of the Assumption of the Blessed Virgin Mary

CCC 411, 966-971, 974-975, 2853: Mary, the New Eve, assumed into heaven
CCC 773, 829, 967, 972: Mary, eschatological icon of the Church
CCC 2673-2679: at prayer with Mary

November 1: The Solemnity of All Saints

CCC 61, 946-962, 1090, 1137-1139, 1370: the Church, a communion of saints
CCC 956, 2683: the intercession of the saints
CCC 828, 867, 1173, 2030, 2683-2684: the saints, examples of holiness

December 8: The Solemnity of the Immaculate Conception of the Blessed Virgin Mary

CCC 411, 489-493, 722, 2001, 2853: God's preparation; the Immaculate Conception

APPENDIX II:

POST-CONCILIAR ECCLESIAL SOURCES RELEVANT TO PREACHING

THE SECOND VATICAN COUNCIL
Constitution on the Sacred Liturgy *Sacrosanctum Concilium*: 7, 24, 35, 52, 56
Dogmatic Constitution on the Church *Lumen Gentium*: 25
Dogmatic Constitution on Divine Revelation *Dei Verbum*: 7-13, 21, 25
Pastoral Constitution on the Church in the Modern World *Gaudium et Spes*: 58
Decree on the Missionary Activity of the Church *Ad Gentes*: 6
Decree on the Ministry and Life of Priests *Presbyterorum Ordinis*: 4, 18

PAPAL MAGISTERIUM
Paul VI
Encyclical *Mysterium Fidei*: 36
Apostolic Exhortation *Evangelii Nuntiandi*: 43, 75-76, 78-79

St John Paul II
Apostolic Exhortation *Catechesi Tradendae*: 48
Apostolic Exhortation *Pastores Dabo Vobis*: 26
Apostolic Exhortation *Pastores Gregis*: 15
Apostolic Letter *Dies Domini*: 39-41
Apostolic Letter *Novo Millennio Ineunte*: 39-40

Benedict XVI
Apostolic Exhortation *Sacramentum Caritatis*: 45-46
Apostolic Exhortation *Verbum Domini*: 52-71

Francis
Apostolic Exhortation *Evangelii Gaudium*: 135-159

LITURGICAL BOOKS

General Instruction of the Roman Missal: 29, 57, 65-66

Introduction of the Lectionary for Mass: 4-31, 38-48, 58-110

Introduction of the Order of Funerals: 15

Introduction of the Rite of Marriage: 22

CODE OF CANON LAW

Canons 762, 767-769

DOCUMENTS OF CONGREGATIONS OF THE ROMAN CURIA

Sacred Congregation of Rites, Instruction *Inter Oecumenici*
(26 November 1964): 53-55

Sacred Congregation of Rites, Instruction *Eucharisticum Mysterium*
(25 May 1967): 10

Congregation for Divine Worship, Instruction *Liturgicae Instaurationes*
(5 September 1970): 2

Congregation for the Clergy, *General Catechetical Directory*
(11 April 1971): 13

Congregation for the Clergy, *Directory for the Ministry and Life of
Priests* (31 January 1994): 45-46

Congregation for Bishops, *Apostolorum Successores*

(22 February 2004): 119-122